OUTDOOR COOKING

PREPARING FOOD THE HEALTHY WAY SERIES

OUTDOOR COOKING

Frederick E. Kahn, M.D.

Nautilus Communications, Inc.
New York, N.Y.

We wish to thank for their contributions and assistance the Cling Peach Advisory Board, Florida Department of Agriculture and Consumer Services, National Pork Producers Council, New Jersey Department of Agriculture, Home Economics Department of the Rice Council and United Fruit and Vegetable Association.

The publisher wishes to thank Scott Grayson and Andrea Spirn for their assistance in the preparation of this book.

Published by Nautilus Communications, Inc.
460 East 79th Street, New York, N.Y. 10021

Design by Kathleen Cronin Tinkel

Cover illustration by Marilyn Ackerman

Printed in the United States of America

Contents

Preface

In recent years attention has been focused on the need for each of us to take control of our own future. The concept of self-help means that we should be able to choose how we act in various situations. One of those areas of choice is nutrition—the process or act of nourishing one's self. Furthermore, the changes in the way we feed ourselves have undergone a revolution.

In today's world, we spend time eating and making choices in ways that are very different from our ancestors. Before the use of cooking, people ate raw foods. Eventually, mankind discovered that cooking would change the taste of food. By the Roman times, emphasis was placed on the enjoyment of food as an activity, and as such, more attention was paid to its preparation. As our modes of transportation changed, different cultures were introduced to foods from other areas of the world. Food preparation, however, remained laborious because of all the activities necessary to make food edible. Preservatives were primitive, at best, and packaging was not in use.

With the advent of industrialization, many changes occurred. First of all food could be transported rapidly over long distances. Refrigeration, packaging, and chemistry allowed food to remain for prolonged periods of time on our shelves. Along with these changes, food preparation has also dramatically changed. Instead of using wood, we've moved to gas and electric methods of cooking as well as using microwaves. Food preparation has speeded up in other areas with the advent of tools and machines to cut and process. Agricultural and technological advances have also added another dimension in producing healthier and more bountiful foodstuffs.

The amount of time we have to spend on ourselves is quite different from what our grandparents had. Because of modern conveniences, along with changes in technology, we have much more leisure time. This allows much more time to follow pursuits other than working. Changes in structure of the family have also made us more isolated and the presence of a nuclear-style family, as well as increasing numbers of adult single individuals have promulgated feelings of loneliness. Food, being one of our earliest contacts with our mothers along with feelings of warmth and wholeness, is a direction that we return to when feeling loneliness. Increasing influence of media has also made us also focus much more on different brands of food as well as how and what we are eating. We are aware that we can do something to improve or prolong our lives through exercise and better nutrition.

Social changes have also played an important role in our changing notions of food—and eating. There have been dramatic alterations in the relationship of an individual to those around him or her. Family structure has changed, and where once the large, sprawling family units were the norm, we have now adopted the smaller, tightly knit "nuclear family" style. There are also many more single adults who make up individual households. In both of these situations we are more likely to experience isolation and feelings of loneliness. Psychologists believe that eating is related to the feeling of warmth and security because of their association during infancy. We often eat when feeling lonely, to replace the lost sensation of wholeness that we experience as babies. When we feel this, we may eat too much or eat improperly.

The choice of what and how much food, where and when to eat, and why we are eating, along with an understanding of nutrition, help us develop the essentials of maintaining good health. Coronary heart disease, obesity, dental caries, iron deficiency anemia, and some types of emotional illnesses result from a lack of attention to what we eat. You may significantly improve your health and increase your life span by being actively concerned about your nutritional intake.

This book will offer you a compendium that is directed toward healthier nutrition. It offers recipes which are designed to reduce excesses of foodstuffs which may lead to poor health. It is not a prescription or formula. I take the attitude that there are many different ways to approach life, and as such, the same is true of our eating habits. Thus, this book presents one of these ways in which you can approach the preparation of food—a healthier way!

What you eat, and how you prepare it, is a decision left to each of you. It is your first step toward a more energetic and healthy life.

Frederick E. Kahn, M.D.

Barbecue and camp-out cooking

Barbecue and camp-out cooking

The first cooking method, roasting on an open fire, is today still one of our most favored techniques. Americans, from the Pilgrims and wagon-train pioneers to the cowboys and mountain men, have had a continuing love affair with the outdoors, and, even today, they have a real fondness for cooking and eating outdoors. Whether cooking with a hibachi in your backyard or with the fire in a pit on a New England beach, it's all the same: a barbecue, good food, good friends, and casual outdoor entertaining.

The food can be as simple as a frankfurter, or as complex as an entire meal. Either way, nearly everyone agrees that everything tastes better when grilled outside. Any meat or fish can be barbecued, and we have divided our book conveniently into these categories. In addition, many accompaniments, snacks, breakfasts, and even desserts can be prepared over the same fire. We have also included an array of salads that make wonderful additions to any grilled meal.

A wide variety of grills are available—from small hibachis to large built-in types. Covered kettles, smokers, and grills fired by gas or electricity can greatly increase and enhance the scope of your cook-out style. All work differently, and you should be familiar with the strengths and limitations of your particular grill.

Aside from the delicious taste advantage of outdoor cooking, this method also gives the cook time away from a hot summer kitchen, provides a fine incentive for a casual party, and allows wonderful food preparations not possible indoors.

Barbecuing is fun, simple and safe if done correctly. Know what you're doing, know what you want, and enjoy yourself.

How to build a barbecue fire

Place dry gravel or crushed rock on the bottom of the fire box. This protects the grill, evenly distributes the heat, and helps prevent flame-ups from drippings. Use a generous amount of briquets made from maple, birch, oak, elm, or other hardwoods. Extinguish any leftover coals after a meal—they can be dried and reused. Use one of the many fire-lighter fluids available, but DO NOT use gasoline or kerosene, and never add fluid once a fire is going. Start the fire early enough to get a sufficiently hot bed of coals. Begin thirty to forty-five minutes before cooking.

Basic barbecue equipment
The grill: Choose a type and size suiting your needs. Shop around for the best one. Meat thermometer.
Gloves: Asbestos-lined or well-padded to prevent burns.
Tools: Long-handled forks, spoons, turners, tongs, and basting brushes.
Knives: They should be sharp for carving and for testing doneness of meat.
Carving board: Not only for carving, but also for cutting and chopping. Choose a strong hardwood block that will withstand wear and tear.
Work space: A table with steady legs.
Skewers: For shish kebabs. Whether fancy or simple, they must be kept clean.
Wire hinged basket: Use to grill fish fillets or shellfish. Makes turning easy.

Basic techniques
Set up your grill according to the manufacturer's directions and requirements of your particular recipe. Grills may employ several different methods of producing heat:

Open grill for direct heat: Layer coals in the fire box so that food can be cooked directly over them. Used for steaks, chops, ribs, burgers, franks, chicken pieces, fish, and shellfish. Also used for rotisserie cooking.

Covered grill for direct heat: Arrange coals as above.

Covered grill for indirect heat: Place a large drip pan made of heavy aluminum foil in the center of the grill under the meat. Arrange coals around it. Used for roasts and poultry. No turning of the meat is necessary.

Spit roasting: An electrical spit or rotisserie should be used according to the manufacturer's directions. Carefully balance the meat or bird on the skewer so that it will rotate smoothly and thus cook uniformly. Readjust skewer if necessary. Station the spit and screw on tightly. Place a pan under the meat to catch the drippings. Baste meats with drippings during the first part of the cooking. Because barbecue sauces burn easily, they should be applied only during the last half or three quarters of an hour.

Meat and poultry should usually be grilled over low, even heat, since that way the meat shrinks less, cooks more uniformly, and does not char. Regulate the heat of the fire by adjusting the number of coals. Allow ten to fifteen coals per pound of meat; add the same number each hour to maintain even heat. Brush salad oil lightly over the grids of the grill before cooking to prevent sticking. Score thick edges of steaks and chops to prevent curling during grilling. Trim fat from edges of meat so that it will not drip onto the coals and cause smoky flareups. For easier handling of fish, hamburgers, and other small foods, place them in a folding, hinged wire grill.

Marinades and sauces enhance the flavor of barbecued meats, fish and poultry. Choose a mild sauce for fish, veal, and poultry. Select heartier ones to accent beef, lamb, or pork. Choose from the numerous commercially bottled products, or make your own sauces following our recipes. Long-cooking foods such as spareribs or chicken should be brushed with tomato-based or sweet sauces during the last twenty minutes of grilling to prevent charring. For a smoky flavor, add wood-chips—apple, hickory, oak, or cherry—to the coals while cooking. Soak the chips in water for an hour or more so that they will provide maximum smoke without burning too quickly.

It is vital to cook meats, fish and poultry for the correct amount of time. This depends not only on the thickness of the meat, but also on the level of heat produced by the grill. A two-inch beef steak, for example, will require twelve to fifteen minutes on each side to turn out medium-rare. Chicken pieces will require forty-five to sixty minutes with frequent turning. A one-pound fish will need about five minutes on each side. When food is ready to turn, use barbecue tongs or a long-handled spatula. Do not use a fork, since it will pierce the meat and allow juices to escape.

Safety precautions

First of all, read the instructions for your particular grill. Always grill outdoors. Since a fire produces carbon monoxide, cooking in enclosed porches or garages can be very dangerous.

Be careful when starting the fire. Use liquid, solid, or semisolid starters according to the label directions. DO NOT use gasoline or kerosene. Or else, begin with woodshavings scattered around the charcoal. Or use an electric starter. Allow plenty of time for coal to reach proper temperature. Start a fire thirty to forty-five minutes ahead of time. Charcoal should be covered with white ash for optimal grilling. For quick-cooking foods, a single layer of briquets is sufficient, while longer-cooking foods need two or more layers. NEVER add lighter fluid to a lit fire.

Test a fire's temperature with a grill thermometer. Or else, count the number of seconds you can hold your hand above the coals: if two seconds or less, the coals are hot (400° F.), three to four seconds, medium-hot (350° F.); five or more seconds, low (300° F.). If the grill is adjustable, you can regulate the height of the rack to get the correct temperature. Moreover, if a grill has a cover and damper, the fire can be adjusted by opening or closing the damper or by covering the top when necessary. While cooking, check temperature occasionally and add more coals if needed.

To prevent flare-ups, tip the rack of an open grill so that drippings run down beyond the coals. Keep a water sprayer handy to douse flare-ups. A drip pan will help prevent flare-ups in a covered grill.

WEIGHTS AND MEASURES

dash — slightly less than ¼ teaspoon
3 teaspoons — 1 tablespoon
2 tablespoons — ⅛ cup — 1 ounce
4 tablespoons — ¼ cup — 2 ounces
5⅓ tablespoons — ⅓ cup
8 tablespoons — ½ cup — 4 ounces
10⅔ tablespoons — ⅔ cup
2 cups — 1 pint — ½ quart — 1 pound
4 cups — 2 pints — 1 quart
4 quarts — 1 gallon
8 dry quarts — 1 peck
4 pecks — 1 bushel

CAN SIZES

8 ounces — 1 cup
12 ounces — 1½ cup
1 pound or 16 ounces — 2 cups
20 ounces — 2½ cups

ABBREVIATIONS

c. — cup(s)
env. — envelope(s)
F. — Fahrenheit
gal. — gallon(s)
in. — inch(es)
med. — medium
min. — minute(s)
oz. — ounce(s)
pkg. — package(s)
pt. — pint(s)
lb. — pound(s)
qt. — quart(s)
sec. — second(s)
T. — tablespoon(s)
t. — teaspoon(s)

Sauces and marinades

Sauces and marinades

These are the foundations of a good barbecue. Since grilling is a dry-heat method of cooking, added moisture and protection from the intense heat are two reasons for using basting sauces. Marinating tenderizes and flavors more economical cuts of meat, and some marinades double as sauces. Most of these recipes are interchangeable and easily adapted to your tastes. Each is distinctive and delicious.

Classic cooked barbecue sauce

¼ c. onions, finely
  chopped
3 T. green onion,
  minced
1 clove garlic, sliced
2 T. butter
2 T. tomato paste
¼ c. salad oil
4 med. tomatoes, peeled,
  seeded, and diced
½ c. beef stock
¼ c. dark brown sugar,
  firmly packed
2 T. prepared mustard
1 T. Worcestershire sauce
1 T. salt
½ t. black pepper

Sauté onions and garlic in butter in a skillet until translucent. Mix in tomato paste, oil, and tomatoes. Cover and simmer for 10 min. Add remaining ingredients; cover, and simmer for 10–15 min., stirring occasionally.

Makes 2 cups.

Classic uncooked barbecue sauce

Quick to make and stores up to a week.

1 c. (8-oz. can) tomato
  sauce
½ c. ketchup
⅓ c. chili sauce
3 T. brown sugar
1 t. dry mustard
1 T. red wine vinegar
2 T. lemon juice
2 T. salad oil
¼ t. garlic powder
1 T. soy sauce
1 t. Worcestershire sauce
¼ t. black pepper

Mix all ingredients thoroughly.

Makes 2 cups.

Speedy BBQ sauce

Best when made a day ahead of time to allow flavors to mellow. Especially good for hamburgers.

1 bottle (12 oz.) chili
   sauce
2 t. celery seeds
3 T. vinegar
1 clove garlic, halved

Combine all ingredients. Chill for several hours. Remove garlic before serving.

Makes 1¼ cups.

Fresh herbed barbecue sauce

3 T. onions, finely
   chopped
3 T. green onions, finely
   chopped
2 cloves garlic, sliced
   thin
4 T. salad oil
3 T. tomato paste
1 c. tomato sauce
½ c. ketchup
2 T. soy sauce
1 t. dry mustard
¼ t. black pepper
2 T. brown sugar
1 T. wine vinegar
1 T. lemon juice
¼ t. celery salt
3 T. parsley, minced
3 T. fresh basil
3 T. tarragon
2 t. thyme, minced
2 bay leaves, finely
   crumbled

Sauté onions and garlic in oil in a skillet until translucent. Mix in remaining ingredients. Simmer for 10 min. Serve hot or cold.

Makes 2 cups

Tangy beef barbecue sauce

4 cloves garlic, finely
   chopped
1 t. sugar
2 T. Tabasco
¾ c. wine vinegar
½ c. soy sauce
¼ c. Worcestershire
   sauce
3 T. ketchup
½ c. olive or salad oil
½ c. beef stock
pepper to taste

Mash garlic into sugar until juicy. Add other ingredients, mix well, and pour over meat. Let stand for several hours. While cooking, baste meat frequently with sauce.

Makes 2½–3 cups.

Mustard sauce for chicken

½ c. butter
1 small onion, minced
1 clove garlic
1½ t. dry mustard
2 T. flour
1½ t. salt
2 T. chili powder
2 c. tomatoes
6 T. lemon juice
½ c. water

Sauté onion and garlic in butter until tender. Add other ingredients and boil for 5 min., or until thick.

Makes 3½–4 cups.

Chili-fruit sauce

Great on ham, pork or shrimp.

1 bottle (14 oz.) ketchup
1 c. pineapple juice
¾ c. green onions,
   chopped
½ t. chili powder

Combine all ingredients in medium bowl.

Makes 1½ cups.

Coffee barbecue sauce

Great for ribs.

1 c. strong black coffee
1½ c. Worcestershire
   sauce
1 c. ketchup
½ c. butter (¼ lb.)
¼ c. lemon juice
2 T. sugar
2 t. cayenne pepper

Mix all ingredients. Simmer for 30 min., stirring occasionally.

Makes 5 cups.

Bacon-tomato barbecue sauce

Especially good on frankfurters or chicken.

6 slices bacon, cooked
   until crisp; fat
   reserved
½ c. onions, minced
½ c. green pepper,
   minced
1 can (10½ oz.)
   condensed tomato
   soup
½ c. water
¼ c. bottled steak sauce
2 t. sugar
1 t. cider vinegar
½ t. salt

Sauté onions and green pepper in 3 tablespoons bacon fat in a skillet until tender (about 5 min.). Stir in remaining ingredients. Simmer, covered, for 15 min., stirring frequently. Add crumbled bacon pieces.

Makes 2 cups.

Aloha sauce

Use on chicken or pork.

¼ c. butter, heated
½ c. catsup
½ c. orange juice
½ c. honey
¼ c. lemon juice
2 T. soy sauce
½ t. ginger

Cook all ingredients in a saucepan over a medium heat, stirring until smooth.

Makes 2 cups.

Sweet-sour mustard sauce

Great on hamburgers or shrimp.

2 T. salad oil
1 small onion, minced
2 T. all-purpose flour
1 c. chicken broth
1 T. sugar
3 T. Dijon mustard
1 t. salt

Sauté onions in hot oil in a saucepan over a medium heat until translucent (about 5 min.). Blend flour into onion, then gradually stir in broth. Add remaining ingredients and cook, stirring constantly, until thickened. Serve hot.

Makes 1 cup.

Lemon-butter sauce

Super with any fish or lobster.

1 c. butter
⅓ c. lemon juice
¼ c. parsley, chopped
1 T. salt
1 T. lemon peel, grated
1 t. sugar
¼ t. pepper

Heat butter in a saucepan over a medium heat. Add remaining ingredients and stir until smooth.

Makes 1½ cups.

Blue-cheese barbecue sauce

Brush on steak or lamb shortly before cooking is finished.

1 T. butter
1 T. all-purpose flour
¾ c. milk
½ c. blue cheese, crumbled
½ t. salt
¼ t. pepper, coarsely ground

Melt butter in a saucepan over a medium heat, then blend in flour. Stir in milk gradually; cook, stirring constantly, until thickened. Remove mixture from stove and blend in remaining ingredients. Serve hot.

Makes 1 cup.

Spicy marinade

Good for lamb and spareribs.

⅓ c. olive oil
2 cloves garlic, crushed
1 t. chili powder
1 t. sugar
1 t. salt
¼ t. pepper
⅓ c. cider vinegar
⅓ c. apple juice

Sauté garlic in hot oil in a saucepan over a medium heat for 2—3 min. Blend in remaining ingredients and stir until smooth. Cool. Baste meat while cooking.

Makes 1 cup.

Easy ginger marinade

Try with shrimp or lamb.

¼ c. soy sauce
2 T. sugar
1 T. garlic salt
1 T. ground ginger
1 bottle (7 oz.) lemon-
   lime soft drink
   (about 1 c.)

Combine ingredients in a bowl.

Makes 1¼ cups.

Fast sweet and sour marinade

Try on game birds or pork.

½ c. oil
1 T. vinegar
1 T. lemon juice
3 T. ketchup

Combine all ingredients in a bowl.

Makes ¾ cup.

Soy-sesame marinade

Especially good on fish or shellfish.

½ c. soy sauce
½ c. onions, minced
2 T. sesame seed
2 T. salad oil
2 t. salt
2 T. light brown sugar
2 t. lemon juice
½ t. pepper
½ t. ginger

Combine ingredients in a bowl.

Makes 1 cup.

Spicy lemon marinade

Light and good on veal, lamb, or chicken.

1 c. olive oil
2 T. lemon juice
1 T. Worcestershire sauce

Combine ingredients in a bowl. Use as a marinade.

Makes about 1 cup.

Garlic marinade

Leave garlic in longer if you like a stronger flavor. Good for whole roasts or flank steak.

4 T. red wine vinegar
1 c. olive oil
2 cloves garlic

Soak garlic in oil overnight. Remove garlic and add vinegar.

Makes 1¼ cup.

Beef and veal

Beef and veal

We have all enjoyed eating a barbecued steak, but what about a marinated chuck roast? A whole spit-roasted rib roast? Succulent short ribs? Extend your repertoire to include these unusual barbecue cuts, as well as tasty veal cooked quickly and easily over an open fire. Almost any cut of beef or veal is a barbecue natural.

Spit-grilled boneless roast

An impressive show, a special dinner.

Buy a 5–6 pound beef rib-eye roast or whole fillet with strings tied at 1½-in. intervals. Place meat securely on spit. Place drip pan under meat. Roast for 2–2½ hours for medium-rare. A cooking thermometer registers 130° F. for rare, 150° F. for medium, and 160° F. for well done. Let stand for 15 min. before carving.

Serve with garlic butter: Simmer 1–2 cloves garlic, mashed, in ½ cup butter for 2 min.

Serves 10–12.

Barbecued or spit-roasted rib roast

For accurate testing, use an instant-read thermometer.

Attach meat according to spit instructions. If roast has adequate fat cover it will need no basting. Meat may also be roasted on the rack, if grill has a cover; leave the vent open. Baste with any marinade. Meat thermometer will register 130° F. for rare and 150° F. for medium.

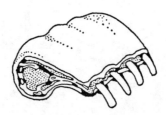

Barbecued pot roast

A tender, tasty method for an economical cut.

round chuck roast 2½
   in. thick (about 3–4
   lb.)
unseasoned meat
   tenderizer
prepared mustard
coarse salt

marinade
¼ c. red wine vinegar
¼ c. brown sugar
½ t. Tabasco
¼ t. oregano

Pierce meat with fork. Sprinkle with tenderizer. Let roast stand in marinade in refrigerator for 5–6 hours. Cook for 20 min. on each side.

Serves 4–6.

Peachy glazed beef brisket

1 fresh boneless beef
   brisket (4½ lb.)
1 medium onion,
   quartered
2 bay leaves
salt
1 can (17 oz.) peach
   halves, drained
2 T. sugar
2 T. cider vinegar
2 T. salad oil
¼ t. ground cloves

Cook brisket, onion, bay leaves, 1 tablespoon salt, and enough water to cover in a covered saucepot. Bring to a boil, then reduce heat and simmer for 2½ hours, until fork-tender. Drain water and discard onions and bay leaves. Remove brisket, cover, and refrigerate overnight. Later, remove meat from refrigerator and prepare outdoor grill. In a blender, put 1 teaspoon salt and remaining ingredients; blend slowly. Grill cooked brisket over medium coals. Cook for 30–40 min., turning a few times. Baste often with peach mixture during final 10 min.

Serves 10–12.

Basic grilled beef steak

Great with a flavored butter topping, or the blue cheese sauce on p. 17.

Select a tender steak 1 to 3-in. thick and streaked with fat. Because they are less tender, cuts such as top round or rump roast should be marinated or tenderized prior to grilling. Cut the fat edge so that the steak will not curl. Rub oil on grate. For medium-rare, grill a 1-in. steak 2 to 3-in. from coals for 5—6 min. on each side. A 2-in. steak will require 10—12 min. on each side. Test by cutting near bone.

Allow 6—8 ounces per serving.

Spiced steaks

½ c. soy sauce
2 T. brown sugar
2 T. Worcestershire
2 T. lemon juice
1 t. salt
4 beef rib or sirloin
   steaks, 1-in. thick

To make marinade, mix first 5 ingredients in a large, shallow baking dish. Place steaks in mixture, cover, and refrigerate for at least 2 hours, flipping steaks a few times. Later, prepare grill. Cook steaks for about 5 min. on each side for rare. Baste frequently with marinade.

Serves 4.

Marinated flank steak

2 T. olive oil
2 T. red wine vinegar
½ clove garlic, mashed
1 flank steak (2 lb.)
¼ t. black pepper,
   freshly ground

Blend oil, vinegar, and garlic and coat steak on both sides. Season with pepper. Pierce with a fork, then pound. Set aside for 30 min. Grill 5-in. from coals, 5 min. on each side for rare. Slice diagonally and thinly.

Serves 4—6.

Lemon chuck steak

Be sure to marinate well for a tender result.

1 boneless chuck steak,
cut 1½ in. thick
(about 4 lb.)
1 t. lemon peel, grated
⅔ c. lemon juice
⅓ c. salad oil
2 t. salt
⅛ t. pepper
1 t. Worcestershire sauce
1 t. Dijon mustard
2 green onion tops,
sliced

Make parallel cuts on fat edges of steaks, then place in a shallow dish. Mix remaining ingredients and pour over meat. Marinate for 3 hours at room temperature (6 hours in refrigerator), turning several times. Remove from marinade and remove excess with paper towels. Grill over hot coals for 12 min. on each side for rare; 15 min. on each side for medium. Brush with marinade occasionally. Slice thinly across grain.

Serves 8.

Steak in a salt crust

The "crust" holds in the natural juices.

1 (2 lb.) boneless sirloin
steak, 2-3 in. thick
2 cloves garlic, cut
pepper to taste
4 c. coarse salt
water

Remove excess fat from steak, then skewer it. Rub each side with garlic. Season with pepper. Mix salt and enough water to make thick paste. Press half of salt paste on top of meat. Place salt-side down over hot coals for 12 min. for rare. Cover other side with salt, turn, and repeat. Before serving, discard salt crust and place steak on a warm deep platter. Pour steak sauce on platter. Slice. Serve with crisp slices of bread to soak up juice.

Serves 2.

Barbecued short ribs

A great treatment for this succulent cut.

3 lb. beef short ribs,
   fat trimmed
1 t. salt
pepper to taste
½ c. water
1 c. chili sauce
1 jar (12 oz.) pineapple
   preserves (1 c.)
⅓ c. vinegar

Season meat with salt and pepper, then place in Dutch oven. Add water, cover, and simmer for about 2 hours, until tender; if necessary, add more water during cooking. Drain liquid. Mix remaining ingredients and coat ribs. Grill over slow coals for 15–20 min.; brush with sauce and turn frequently.

Serves 3–4.

Chuck kebobs

Add some parboiled new potatoes to the skewer for a whole meal on a stick.

½ pkg. (¼ c.) dry
   onion soup mix
2 T. sugar
½ c. ketchup
¼ c. vinegar
¼ c. salad oil
1 t. dry mustard
¼ t. salt
dash of Tabasco sauce
½ c. water
1½ lb. beef chuck, cut
   in 1-in. cubes
instant unseasoned meat
   tenderizer
1 green pepper, cut in
   chunks
1 sweet red pepper, cut
   in chunks

Mix first 9 ingredients in a saucepan and bring to a boil. Lower heat, simmer 20 min., then cool slightly. Add meat chunks and toss to coat. Refrigerate overnight. Drain meat, reserving marinade. Use tenderizer on meat, following label directions. Alternate meat chunks and pepper on skewers. Grill over medium coals for 20–25 min., turning once and brushing with marinade several times. Serve remaining heated marinade as sauce.

Serves 4.

Teriyaki kebobs

½ c. soy sauce
¼ c. salad oil
2 T. molasses
2 t. ground ginger
2 t. dry mustard
6 cloves garlic, minced
1½ lbs. chuck or round
   steak, 1-in. thick
instant unseasoned meat
   tenderizer
2 c. canned pineapple
   chunks, drained

Mix first 6 ingredients for marinade. Slice meat in ¼-in. strips. Use tenderizer on meat following label directions. Place meat in marinade, stir to coat, and let stand for 15 min. Skewer meat strips accordion-style; add pineapple to skewer ends. Grill over hot coals for 5–7 min., turning frequently and basting with marinade.

Serves 6.

Beef kebobs with 3 sauces

Next time, try some other sauce combinations.

2 sirloin steaks, 1½ in.
   thick (3–4 lb. each),
   trimmed and cut
   into 1½-in. cubes
   (36–40)
1 c. classic cooked
   barbecue sauce
   (p. 12)
1 c. fresh herbed
   barbecue sauce
   (p. 13)
1 c. aloha sauce (p. 16)

Pour basic cooked barbecue sauce over cubes of beef in a bowl. Stir well. Let stand for at least 2 hours. Affix meat to 6 long skewers, wiping off excess sauce to prevent charring. Grill 4-in. from hot coals for 15–18 min. for medium-rare; turn often. Baste each sauce generously on 2 skewers toward end of cooking time. Or else baste each skewer with all 3 sauces in adjacent areas.

Serves 6–8.

Basic grilled veal steak

Veal is excellent on the grill!

Veal steaks cut from the leg, 1–1½ in. thick, require long cooking. Grill them slowly over a moderate heat. Brush with sauce of choice.

Allow 1 steak per person.

Barbecued veal chops

Use chops about 1–1½-inches thick.

Veal rib, shoulder, or loin chops can be seasoned and marinated like lamb chops. Veal is more flavorful and more tender when marinated and then basted with the marinade during cooking. Use marinade of choice. Cook through for maximum tenderness. Thicker cuts should be grilled 8-in. from coals, thinner cuts 5-in.

Allow 1 chop per person.

Pork and ham

Pork and ham

There is hardly a barbecue sauce or marinade known that doesn't go well with pork. From the classic chops and barbecued ribs of Texas to the whole pig roast of a luau in Hawaii, pork is a most popular cookout fare. Ham is a versatile, tasty barbecue entrée, and since most ham is already cooked, it needs only a quick heating and saucing.

Sassy barbecued pork

2 c. sugar
1 c. soy sauce
¼ c. beef stock
¼ c. red wine vinegar
½ c. chili sauce
1 t. ground cinnamon
1 clove garlic, minced
3–4 lb. boneless pork
loin roast (double
loin, rolled and tied)

Mix first 6 ingredients. Place roast in a heavy plastic bag, pour marinade over roast and tie bag securely. Marinate overnight in refrigerator, turning meat occasionally. Make an aluminum foil drip pan 1½-in. deep and extending 3-in. beyond each side of meat; place under rotisserie. Place roast on rotisserie of grill over low coals. Insert meat thermometer in thickest part of roast, not touching fat. Close hood. Cook for about 2 hours, or until meat thermometer registers 170° F. Baste frequently with marinade during last hour of grilling. Let roast stand for 15 min. before carving to allow juices to set.

Serves 8–12.

Spit-roasted peanut-orange pork

Wonderful served with grilled peaches and a green salad.

4–5 lb. boned pork loin
roast, rolled and tied
salt and pepper to taste
½ c. orange juice
¼ c. creamy peanut
butter

Secure roast on spit and insert meat thermometer. Sprinkle with salt and pepper. Place medium coals at rear of firebox; arrange an aluminum foil drip pan under roast in front of coals. With hood lowered, grill to interior temperature of 170° F., about 3 hours. Mix orange juice and peanut butter, brush on roast, and continue cooking and basting for 20 min.

Serves 10–12.

Basic barbecued pork chops

Loin chops are expensive but worth every penny. Select chops 1–2 in. thick for optimum flavor and juiciness. Season with salt and freshly ground black pepper. Grill slowly over medium coals. To be sure chops are cooked through, they should be grilled for at least ½ hour on each side.

Allow 1–2 chops per serving.

Molasses apple pork chops

1½ c. apple cider
¼ c. lemon juice
¼ c. soy sauce
2 T. molasses
1 clove garlic, minced
¼ t. pepper
4 pork loin chops (8 oz. each), 1-in. thick

Combine all ingredients except pork chops; mix well. Place chops in a shallow dish and pour marinade over them. Cover and refrigerate overnight, turning meat occasionally. Remove from marinade. Grill meat 6-in. above low to medium coals for 40–50 min. Turn and baste with marinade every 10–15 min.

Serves 4.

Grilled pepper pork chops

A subtle, peppery flavor.

2 cloves garlic, crushed
1 T. crushed coriander seeds
3 peppercorns, crushed
2 t. brown sugar
3 T. soy sauce
4 pork loin chops, 1-in. thick

Combine all ingredients except pork chops. Brush chops generously with marinade. Cover and set aside for 30 min., brushing occasionally with marinade. Grill meat 5–6 in. above medium coals for 8–10 min. on each side. Brush with marinade and grill an additional 10 to 12 min., brushing occasionally with marinade.

Serves 4.

Grilled pineapple pork chops

chili fruit sauce (p. 14)
6 thick pork chops
6 slices canned
   pineapple
butter, melted
2 T. dark brown sugar
powdered cloves

Marinate chops in chili fruit sauce for 2 hours. Grill meat 8-in. above coals, basting often and turning frequently. Cook until chops are browned and cooked thoroughly, but not dry. Heat pineapple slices on grill, brush with butter, sprinkle with sugar and cloves, and heat until sugar melts. Serve pineapple atop chops.

Serves 6.

Maple pork steaks

4 pork shoulder blade
   steaks (12 oz. each),
   about 1–1¼ in. thick
½ c. commercial
   barbecue sauce
⅓ c. maple syrup
1 T. soy sauce
1 t. garlic salt
½ t. pepper
½ t. prepared mustard

Tenderize steaks by pounding with meat mallet. Combine remaining ingredients; mix well. Grill meat 4-in. above low coals for 20 min. on each side. Brush with sauce and continue cooking for 10–20 min., turning and basting occasionally. Heat remaining sauce and serve with steaks, if desired.

Serves 4.

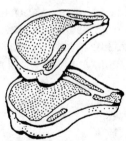

Sweet-sour pork kebobs

½ c. unsweetened
    pineapple juice
¼ c. soy sauce
¼ c. green onions with
    tops, sliced
4 t. sesame seeds
1 T. brown sugar
1 clove garlic, minced
⅛ t. pepper
1½ lb. boneless pork,
    cut in 16 cubes
1 t. cornstarch
2 T. cold water
1 medium red pepper,
    cut in 1-in. squares
12 medium fresh
    mushrooms

Combine pineapple juice, soy sauce, green onions, sesame seeds, sugar, garlic, and pepper in a large bowl; mix well. Add pork, cover, and refrigerate overnight, turning meat occasionally. Drain meat, reserving marinade. Blend cornstarch and water in a medium saucepan. Add reserved marinade; cook and stir over a medium heat until thickened. Alternate red peppers, marinated meat, and mushrooms on 4 skewers. Place on grill 6-in. above medium coals. Cook for 15–20 min., turning once and brushing with sauce occasionally.

Serves 4.

Herbed and spiced country ribs

4 lb. pork country-style
    ribs, or back ribs, cut
    in serving pieces
1 can (15 oz.) tomato
    sauce
¾ c. light brown sugar,
    packed
½ c. red wine vinegar
1 T. salt
1 T. celery seed
1 T. chili powder
2 t. garlic salt
2 t. oregano leaves
1 t. pepper
½ t. ground cloves
pinch of nutmeg

Place ribs in water to cover in a large saucepan. Bring to a boil over a high heat. Lower heat, cover, and simmer for 1 hour. Drain, remove ribs, cover, and refrigerate overnight. An hour before serving, remove ribs from refrigerator and prepare grill for barbecuing. Combine all ingredients except ribs in a bowl or saucepan. Grill ribs over medium coals for 30 min., or until fork-tender. Baste generously with sauce, turning often, during final 20 min.

Serves 4.

Basic barbecued spareribs

Here are three basic techniques.

To spit-barbecue ribs, lace them accordion-style on a spit. Slip one spit fork on the spit rod and start with the narrow end of the ribs and lace. Repeat this operation until all ribs are on the rod. Bring all ribs to the center of the rod and push together, slip the second spit fork on rod and tighten screws on both forks with pliers. Run skewers through ribs to hold on rod securely. Cook for at least 45 min. for heat to be evenly distributed. Baste constantly. Don't allow flames to touch meat. Keep a pail of water handy to avoid flame-ups.

To barbecue ribs on the grill, turn them every 2 min. until they shrink from the ends, which means they are done. Be sure to baste constantly, or ribs will dry out.

Or, parcook ribs for 1 hour in simmering water to cover or in a foil-covered pan in a 300° F. oven. Drain well, then finish on grill for about 20 min., brushing often with sauce of choice.

When ribs are done, immediately slice them apart. Put them on aluminum foil and brush with barbecue sauce. Have plenty of napkins handy.

Allow about 1 pound per person.

Easy peachy ribs

Next time try strained apricots or pineapple.

2 (4½ oz.) jars strained
   peaches (baby food)
⅓ c. ketchup
⅓ c. vinegar
2 T. soy sauce
½ c. brown sugar
1 clove garlic, minced
2 t. ground ginger
1 t. salt
dash of pepper
4 lb. meaty spareribs

Combine first 9 ingredients; mix well. Rub ribs with additional salt and pepper. Grill ribs bone-side down over slow coals for 20 min. Turn once and grill for 10 min., or until browned. Turn meat again, brush with sauce, and broil, without turning, for 30 min. or until meat is well done. Baste often with sauce.

Serves 4–6.

Ruby spareribs

4 lb. pork spareribs, cut in 2- or 3-rib portions
1 jar (10 oz.) red currant jelly
½ c. lemon juice
3 T. cornstarch
1 T. salt
1 T. lemon peel, grated
1 clove garlic, minced
pinch of cinnamon

Place ribs in water to cover in a large saucepan. Bring to a boil over a high heat, then reduce heat, cover and simmer for 1 hour. Drain, remove ribs, cover, and refrigerate overnight. An hour before serving, remove ribs from refrigerator and prepare grill for barbecuing. Mix remaining ingredients in a saucepan over a medium heat. Cook until mixture thickens and jelly melts, stirring constantly. Grill ribs over medium coals for 20 min. until tender. Baste often with sauce and turn occasionally.

Serves 4.

Barbecued fresh ham

Since ham must cook slowly, do not make the fire too hot. Season meat with salt and pepper, and rub garlic on it. Make sauce by mixing 1 cup orange juice, ½ cup lemon juice, and 1 cup salad oil. Roast the ham slowly on the spit, basting often with sauce. Allow about 30 min. per pound for meat to reach internal temperature of 185° F. Be sure it is thoroughly cooked.

Allow ⅓– ½ pound of bone-in ham per person.

Ham 'n' sweet kebobs

2 ham steaks, ¾-in. thick, cut in squares
6 small sweet potatoes, cooked, peeled, and cut in chunks
1 can (29 oz.) peach halves, drained
½ c. butter, melted
¼ c. brown sugar

On skewers, alternate pieces of ham, sweet potatoes, and peaches. Roll in butter. Grill close to coals until potatoes brown. Sprinkle with sugar and butter. Grill until glazed.

Serves 8.

Spit-roasted ham with currant-apple glaze

Great with potato salad for a crowd.

1 boneless ham, fully
    cooked, 4–5 lb.
1 jar (10 oz.) apple jelly
1 jar (10 oz.) currant
    jelly
1 T. lemon juice
1 t. cinnamon

Place ham on rotisserie skewer following manufacturer's directions; place drip pan under meat. Insert thermometer into center of ham at a slant so that dial is close to 1 end. Heat jellies, lemon juice, and cinnamon in a small saucepan over a low heat, stirring until jellies melt. Grill ham on rotisserie for 1½ hours or until thermometer reads 130° F. Baste during final 15 min. with currant-apple glaze. Let stand 15 min. before serving for easier carving. Serve remaining glaze in a separate dish.

Serves 16–20.

Apricot ham slice

Quick and easy for a small party.

½ c. ketchup, heated
⅓ c. apricot preserves
2 T. onions, finely
    chopped
2 T. salad oil
1 T. lemon juice
1½ t. dry mustard
1 slice cooked ham
    (about 1-in. and 1½
    lb.)

Mix all ingredients except ham. Score fat edge of ham. Grill over slow coals for 15 min., turning once. Baste with sauce. Grill for 15 min. more, turning and basting once. Warm sauce on edge of grill, then serve it with ham.

Serves 4.

Ballpark ham slice

Cut up the cooked ham and serve in hot dog buns if you wish.

½ c. ketchup
⅓ c. sweet pickle relish
1 T. cider vinegar
⅛– ¼ t. cayenne
   pepper
1 slice cooked ham (2
   lb.)

Mix first 4 ingredients in a small saucepan. Grill ham slice over medium coals for 20 min. until heated through. Baste frequently with sauce and turn occasionally.

Serves 6.

Hawaiian ham kebobs

1 boneless ham, cooked,
   2– 2½ lb. and cut in
   1½-in. cubes
1 can (29 oz.) pineapple
   chunks
3– 4 oranges, unpeeled,
   seeded, and cut in
   wedges
½ c. chili sauce
⅓ c. orange marmalade
2 T. onions, finely
   chopped
2 T. salad oil
1 T. lemon juice
1½ t. dry mustard

On skewers, alternate ham chunks and fruits. Combine remaining ingredients. Grill ham and fruits over low coals for 12– 15 min. Rotate often and brush frequently with sauce.

Serves 6.

Burgers and sausages

Burgers and sausages

Here are some classic cookout treats, including the classic grilled hamburgers and the skewered hot dogs of beach picnics. But don't stop there! Try your next burger with ground pork, stuff your hot dog, or even frost and grill a piece of bologna or salami. These low-cost meats make super cookout meals.

Seasoned burgers

The ketchup and mustard are in the burgers.

1 lb. ground beef
¼ c. onions, chopped
3 T. ketchup
1 T. prepared
 horseradish
1 t. salt
2 t. prepared mustard
dash of pepper
2 T. pickle relish

Mix all ingredients and form 4 patties (½-in. thick). Grill over hot coals for 5 min., turn, and broil for 3 min. more.

Serves 4.

California goat-cheese burgers

The height of the new American cooking!

2 lb. lean ground beef
⅓ c. onions, chopped
⅓ c. crumbled goat
 cheese
2 t. salt
1 T. Worcestershire sauce
½ c. butter, softened
¼ c. Dijon mustard
16 slices sourdough
 bread (½-in. thick
 each)

Mix first 5 ingredients and shape into 8 patties. Mix butter and mustard and spread generously on 1 side of bread slices. Reassemble loaf, buttered sides back-to-back, wrap in foil, and place on grill for 15 min. Grill burgers 8 min., turn, and broil 4–7 min. more. Serve between bread slices.

Serves 8.

Grilled burgers Roma

Like a barbecued pizza.

1 lb. ground beef,
  shaped in 4 patties
4 slices mozzarella
  cheese
4 T. spaghetti sauce
2 T. Parmesan cheese

Grill burgers on 1 side, turn, top with a slice of mozzarella, a spoonful of sauce, and Parmesan cheese, and grill until done. Serve on toasted garlic bread.

Serves 4.

Basil and parsley burgers

The topping also makes a great veggie or chip dip.

1 c. sour cream
1 t. prepared mustard
3 T. fresh basil
3 T. parsley, chopped
1½ lb. ground beef
salt and pepper to taste

Combine first 4 ingredients. Shape meat into 6 patties (½-in. thick). Grill over hot coals for 9 min. Turn, sprinkle with salt and pepper, and grill for 6 min. longer or as desired. Serve on toasted buns and top with sauce.

Serves 6.

Pita burgers

1 lb. ground beef
½ t. salt
dash of pepper
4 T. feta or blue cheese,
  crumbled
onions, chopped
barbecue sauce

Mix beef, salt, and pepper and shape into 8 patties (¼-in. thick). Place cheese, onions, and dash of barbecue sauce in center of 4 patties. Top each with another patty and press edges to seal. Grill over hot coals for 12–15 min., turning once. Serve in pita bread.

Serves 4.

Burger Niçoise

Like the famous French Riviera salad. Serve with boiled potatoes and green beans.

1½ lb. ground chuck
⅓ c. Parmesan cheese, grated
¼ c. onions, finely chopped
⅓ c. ripe olives, pitted and chopped
1 t. anchovy paste
1 t. salt
dash of pepper
1 t. dried oregano, crushed
1 can (6 oz.) tomato paste
4 slices Fontina cheese, cut in strips
8 tomatoes, sliced
8 slices French bread, toasted

Mix first 9 ingredients and form 8 patties. Grill over medium coals for 10 min., turn, and top with cheese and tomatoes. Grill for 5 min. more or as desired. Serve open-face on toasted French bread.

Serves 8.

BBQ meat loaves

2 lb. ground beef
2 eggs, slightly beaten
2 c. soft bread crumbs
¼ c. onions, finely chopped
1 T. prepared horseradish
1½ t. salt
½ t. dry mustard
¼ c. milk
1 c. bacon tomato barbecue sauce (p. 15)

Mix first 8 ingredients and form 6 miniature loaves about 4½ x 2½-in. Brush sauce over loaves. Grill over medium coals. Frequently turn and brush all sides with sauce. Grill for 40 min. or until done. Serve with remaining sauce.

Serves 6.

Bacon pork burgers

Be sure to cook these to medium-well done.

2 lb. lean ground pork
1 medium green pepper,
  finely chopped
1 medium onion, finely
  chopped
½ c. vinegar
¼ c. brown sugar, firmly
  packed
2 T. soy sauce
1½ t. seasoned salt
1 t. garlic salt
½ t. pepper
8 slices bacon

Combine first 9 ingredients, mix well, and shape into 8 patties. Wrap with bacon and secure with a wooden toothpick. Grill patties about 6-in. above medium to medium-high coals. Cook for 20–25 min. on each side or until done.

Serves 8.

Campfire dogs

4 plump frankfurters
4 long strips Cheddar
  cheese
4 slices bacon
4 frankfurter rolls

Split franks halfway and insert cheese. Wrap bacon slice around each frank and secure with a toothpick. Place on toasting fork or long green stick and toast until franks are cooked and bacon crisp. Serve on toasted roll.

Serves 4.

Barbecue hamdogs

1 c. cooked ham, finely
   chopped
3 T. pickle relish
2 T. onions, finely
   chopped
2 T. prepared mustard
2 T. mayonnaise
8 frankfurters (1 lb.)
8 slices bacon
bottled barbecue sauce

Blend first 5 ingredients. Slit franks ¾ through and
almost to ends. Pack with ham mixture, wrap each
with a bacon slice and secure with a toothpick. Grill
over hot coals, basting with sauce, until filling is hot
and bacon crisp. Serve in toasted buns.

Serves 8.

Sunshine franks

Serve with baked beans.

1 c. orange marmalade
½ (8 oz.) can tomato
   sauce (½ c.)
⅓ c. vinegar
2 T. orange juice
2 T. lemon juice
2 T. soy sauce
2 T. honey
1 T. salad oil
1 t. salt
¼ t. ground ginger
16 frankfurters (2 lb.),
   scored

Mix first 10 ingredients. Grill franks over hot coals,
turning and basting often with sauce. Serve with
remaining sauce.

Serves 8–12.

Chili dogs

½ lb. lean ground beef
1 c. canned tomatoes
1 clove garlic, minced
1 t. chili powder
salt and pepper to taste
8 frankfurters (1 lb.)
8 buns
½ c. onions, chopped

Brown beef, stirring with a fork, then add tomatoes, garlic, and chili powder, cover, and simmer for 20 min. Add salt, pepper, and more chili powder, if desired. Pour sauce over grilled franks on rolls. Garnish with onions.

Serves 8.

Campfire dogs and beans

1½ lb. fresh green beans
1 can (15 oz.) tomato
  sauce
1 can (6 or 8½ oz.)
  water chestnuts,
  drained
¼ c. brown sugar,
  packed lightly
2 T. bottled steak sauce
1½ t. salt
8 frankfurters (1 lb.),
  halved

Mix first 6 ingredients in a skillet (if skillet's handle is not metal, keep it away from direct heat of grill). Place franks over bean mixture, cover, and cook over medium coals for 15–20 min. until beans are tender. Stir occasionally.

Serves 4–6.

Frosted salami

1 lb. whole salami
½ c. pasteurized cheese
  spread
¼ c. Dijon mustard
buns, toasted

Place whole salami on a spit. Mix cheese and mustard and spread on all sides of meat. Grill over hot coals until browned. Slice and serve on toasted buns. Serve with sauce.

Serves 6–8.

Bologna kebobs

The cheese melts into the bologna wrapper.

8 large slices bologna
2 T. prepared mustard
8 cubes Swiss cheese
(½-in.)
8 slices dill pickle
¼ c. bottled Italian
salad dressing

Spread mustard on bologna. Top each slice with cheese cube and pickle. Fold in quarters, insert toothpick to hold together, and thread on skewer. Grill over hot coals for 10 min. or until lightly browned; turn and brush frequently with dressing.

Serves 4.

Sausage fruit kebobs

1 lb. brown-and-serve
sausages
1 can apricot halves (16
oz.)
2 apples, cored and
thickly sliced
butter, melted

Alternate sausages, apricots, and apples on skewers. Brush generously with butter. Grill 4–5 in. over coals for 5 min. on each side until done.

Serves 4.

Bologna kebobs

1 lb. whole bologna, cut
in 16 chunks
1 can (16 oz.) small
whole onions, drained
2 green peppers,
quartered
¾ c. classic cooked
barbecue sauce
(p. 12)

Alternate bologna, onions, and peppers on 4 skewers. Grill over low coals for 15 min. or until done. Turn kebobs occasionally and baste frequently with sauce.

Serves 4.

All-in-one sausage dinner

Easy on a picnic or camping trip.

2 lb. smoked sausage,
  cut in chunks
1 pkg (2 lb.) frozen
  hash-brown potatoes
1 medium onion,
  chopped
3 stalks celery, thinly
  sliced
1½ t. salt

Brown sausage in a skillet over medium coals. Drain on paper towels and keep warm. Discard all but ⅓ cup of drippings from skillet; then add frozen potatoes and remaining ingredients. Cook for 20 min., until potatoes are browned and celery tender. Turn mixture occasionally with spatula. Add sausage. Serve from skillet.

Serves 8.

Tuna burgers

½ c. onions, chopped
¼ c. oil from tuna, or
  butter
⅓ c. water or clam juice
⅓ c. dry bread crumbs
2 eggs, beaten
¼ c. parlsey, chopped
1 t. powdered mustard
½ t. salt
2 (7½ oz.) cans tuna in
  oil, drained (reserve
  liquid) and flaked
½ c. dry bread crumbs
⅓ c. mayonnaise
1 T. sweet pickles,
  chopped
6 hamburger rolls,
  buttered

Sauté onions in 2 tablespoons oil until tender. Add water, bread crumbs, eggs, parsley, mustard, salt, and tuna. Mix well and form 6 patties. Roll patties in remaining crumbs. Fry in remaining oil in a heavy frying pan about 4 in. from hot coals for 3 min. Turn carefully and fry for another 3 min. or until brown. Drain on paper towels. Blend mayonnaise and pickles. Place burgers in rolls and top with mayonnaise mixture.

Serves 6.

Lamb

Lamb

In ancient times lamb was a sacrificial offering—thus lamb is one of the oldest cookout meats. It also happens to be one of the most succulent and delicious of barbecue treats. From quick and easy chops to a whole spit-roasted leg, these dishes will find favor with even a diehard lamb-hater.

Basic barbecued leg of lamb

To spit-barbecue a leg of lamb (whole leg, boned and rolled leg, or shoulder), first rub it with salt, coarse pepper, and garlic. Center it on a spit rod and insert a meat thermometer in the thickest part. Baste with any barbecue sauce. Allow 25–30 min. per pound. Cook to an internal temperature of 170° F.

A 6-pound leg will serve 8.

Mustard barbecued lamb

Easy and tangy.

1 c. oil
1 clove garlic, minced
4 T. prepared coarse-grain mustard
1 leg of lamb, trimmed for roasting

Blend first 3 ingredients and then spread on lamb. Let stand overnight, turning occasionally. Center meat on spit and roast. Baste occasionally with marinade.

Herbed butterfly leg of lamb

1–2 cloves garlic, minced
1 t. salt
½ t. basil
½ t. oregano
½ t. pepper
½ t. dried thyme, crushed
¼ c. onions, grated
½ c. olive oil
½ c. red wine vinegar
1 leg of lamb (5–6 lb.), boned and butterflied

Mix first 9 ingredients in a large dish or baking pan. Set lamb in marinade for at least 1 hour at room temperature, or overnight in the refrigerator; turn occasionally. Reserve marinade. For easy turning, insert 2 long skewers through meat at right angles or place in a wire basket. Grill over medium coals for 1½–2 hours. Turn every 15 min. and baste frequently with marinade. Slice thinly across the grain.

Serves 8.

Basic grilled lamb chops and steaks

Select loin, rib, or shoulder chops or lamb steaks cut from the leg, all 1½–2 in. thick. Marinate if desired. Season. Grill on rack set 5-in. over coals for 7–8 min. on each side for medium-rare. Cook longer, if desired, but do not overcook.

Allow 1–2 chops per person.

Grilled marinated lamb chops

¾ c. olive oil
1 clove garlic, minced
1 t. dried rosemary
3 T. lemon juice
6 thick lamb chops

Mix first 4 ingredients and brush on both sides of chops. Let stand for 1 hour before grilling.

Serves 6.

Minted lamb chops

The marinade forms a lovely sauce. Serve with buttered new potatoes.

2 T. Worcestershire
   sauce
2 T. butter
2 T. lemon juice
2 T. cider vinegar
black pepper to taste
1 T. mint, freshly
   chopped
6 thick lamb chops, fat
   trimmed, kidney
   reserved
½ c. mint jelly

Heat all ingredients, except chops and jelly, and coat on both sides of chops. Let stand for 30 min. Grill. Heat remaining marinade, add jelly, and serve as sauce.

Serves 6.

Lamb shish kebob

These take only a short while to cook.

1 c. wine vinegar
½ t. cinnamon
½ t. cloves
1 onion, chopped
1 clove garlic, chopped
½ c. olive oil
½ c. vegetable oil
1 leg of lamb (2 lb.), in
   1½-in. cubes
8–12 tomato wedges
8–12 mushrooms
8–12 small new
   potatoes, parboiled

Heat vinegar and spices. Cool. Mix in onion, garlic, and oils. Place in a bowl and add lamb, turning to coat. Let stand for 2 hours at room temperature, turning occasionally. Alternate lamb cubes and vegetables on skewers. Brush with marinade. Grill 3 in. over coals until crusty on outside and medium-rare inside.

Serves 8.

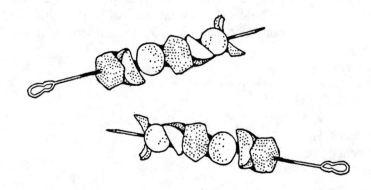

Grecian lamb kebobs

Serve with toasted pita bread and a rice salad.

½ c. salad oil
¼ c. lemon juice
1 t. salt
1 t. dried marjoram,
   crushed
1 t. dried rosemary,
   crushed
½ t. pepper
1 clove garlic, minced
½ c. onions, chopped
¼ c. parsley, snipped
2 lb. boneless lamb, cut
   in 1½-in. cubes
green peppers,
   quartered
sweet red peppers,
   quartered
onion wedges, cooked

Mix first 9 ingredients, add lamb, and stir to coat. Refrigerate for several hours or overnight, turning occasionally. Alternate lamb cubes, red and green pepper, and onion on skewers. Broil over hot coals for 10–12 min. Turn frequently and brush often with marinade.

Serves 6.

Poultry

Poultry

What could be better on the Fourth of July than a huge platter of messy, dripping-with-goodness barbecued chicken? That's only the beginning, however. Try an elegant feast of roasted whole Cornish hens or a sophisticated smoked turkey. A chicken in every pot may turn into a duck on every grill after you try some of these recipes.

Basic barbecued whole poultry

Plump roasting chickens, small hen turkeys, or capons can be spit-roasted. Sprinkle salt and pepper inside and out. Truss. Place on spit. Brush with melted butter or any barbecue sauce (see pp. 12–17). Baste frequently. Grill for 1–3 hours, depending on size. Poultry is usually done when the drumstick moves easily. To be sure, test with an instant-reading thermometer inserted in the thickest part of the breast.

A 4½–5 pound chicken serves 4.

Basic smoked turkey

This slow method gives an outstanding flavor. Use hickory, apple, or mesquite chips.

1 turkey (14–16 lb.)
1 T. salt
butter, melted

Rub inside of bird with salt. Skewer neck skin to back. Balance on spit and anchor with holding forks. Tie wings against body and legs to tail. Brush bird with butter. Place medium-slow coals at back and sides of grill. Arrange a foil-covered drip pan under turkey. Cook with hood lowered for 5–5½ hours. Throw damp hickory chips over coals every 20–30 min. Brush occasionally with butter.

Serves 8–10.

Barbecued turkey with orange-pecan glaze

Use the glaze with duck or Cornish hens, too.

1 frozen, ready-to-stuff
  prebasted turkey,
  thawed
butter, melted
1 c. orange marmalade
½ c. pecans, finely
  chopped
3 T. lemon juice
3 T. onions, minced
2 t. salt

Remove giblets and neck from inside turkey. Rinse and drain bird. Fold wing tips flat under the back to balance turkey. Tie drumsticks together with string across tail, or push drumsticks under band of skin, or use stuffing clamps. Brush bird with butter. Insert thermometer into thick part of thigh; it should not touch bone. Mix last 5 ingredients in a saucepan over a medium heat until marmalade melts.

Prepare grill for indirect-heat method. Arrange drip pan. Place turkey directly on grill or on rotisserie. Cover. Roast for 2½–3 hours, adding coals as needed. During last 15 min., baste with glaze. Cook until thermometer reads 180°–185° F., or when drumstick feels soft. Remove from grill and let stand for 15 min. for easier carving.

Serves 16.

Basic grilled game birds

Whole or split Rock Cornish hens should be cooked on a rotisserie, or split in half and cooked directly on the grill like frying chickens. Whole hens take about 1–1¼ hours; halves about 40–45 min.

Allow ½–1 hen per serving.

Lemon game hens

4 (1 lb.) Cornish game
  hens
salt
1 can (20 oz.) pineapple
  chunks, drained
¾ c. lemon butter sauce
  (p. 17)

Rinse hens; dry with paper toweling. Lightly sprinkle salt inside and stuff with pineapple. Truss. Tie cavity closed. Mount crosswise on spit, alternating their direction, and secure with holding forks. Birds should not be touching. Brush with sauce. Grill over medium coals for 1–1¼ hours, or until done. Brush with sauce 4–5 times.

Serves 4.

Ginger soy chicken

1 c. salad oil
⅓ c. lemon juice
3 T. soy sauce
1 t. Worcestershire sauce
1 clove garlic, minced
2 t. fresh ginger root,
  minced
1 t. salt
¼ t. pepper
6 chicken halves

Combine all ingredients except chicken. Marinate chicken in mixture for 4–5 hours in refrigerator. Baste with sauce while grilling.

Serves 6–8.

Barbecued stuffed chicken breasts

4 oz. ham, finely
  chopped
1 c. seasoned dry bread
  crumbs
2 T. onions, grated
½ t. poultry seasoning
4 whole chicken breasts,
  split and boned
salt to taste
butter or margarine,
  melted

Mix first 4 ingredients thoroughly. Spoon mixture in center of breasts, roll up, and tie or skewer. Season with salt and brush with butter. Roast on greased grill for 30–45 min. Turn and brush with butter every 15 min.

Serves 6–8.

Plum barbecued chicken

Next time use apricots or nectarines.

1 broiler-fryer (2½‒3
   lb.), quartered
salad oil, melted butter,
   or margarine
2 t. salt
¼ t. pepper
¼ c. light corn syrup
4 plums, pitted
¼ t. cinnamon
pinch of nutmeg

Brush chicken with oil and season with salt and pepper. Mix remaining ingredients in blender at low speed until plums are pureed. Grill chicken over medium coals for 45 min. or until fork-tender. Turn occasionally. During final 5 min., baste often with sauce.

Serves 4.

Chili marinated drumsticks

Also good on chicken wings.

¼ c. chili sauce
2‒3 T. lemon juice
2 T. soy sauce
¼ c. salad oil
12 chicken drumsticks

Mix first 4 ingredients thoroughly. Add drumsticks and turn to coat. Refrigerate overnight, stirring occasionally. Grill chicken in wire broiler basket over medium coals for 1 hour, or until tender. Turn and baste with marinade occasionally.

Serves 6.

Marinated grilled turkey parts

Quicker than a whole turkey and no carving is needed!

1 ready-to-cook turkey
(6–7 lb.)
¼ c. salad oil
¼ c. soy sauce
2 T. maple syrup
1 t. ground ginger
1 t. dry mustard
1 clove garlic, minced
2 T. onions, minced

Cut turkey in 12 pieces—2 wings, 2 drumsticks, 2 thighs, 4 breast pieces, and 2 back pieces. Mix remaining ingredients. Add turkey pieces and turn to coat. Marinate for 2 hours at room temperature or overnight in refrigerator. Grill 6–8 in. above medium-hot coals for 30 min., turning occasionally. Add wings and back and broil for another 30 min. Baste with marinade and cook for a final 30 min. Test doneness by cutting into drumstick; meat should not be pink near bone.

Serves 10–12.

Chicken teriyaki

½ c. soy sauce
¼ c. sherry
¼ c. sugar
1 T. slivered candied
ginger, or ½ t.
powdered ginger
2 cloves garlic, minced
3 lb. boneless chicken
breasts, cut in thin
slices across grain

Combine first 5 ingredients. Place chicken pieces in sauce for 1 hour at room temperature. Skewer accordion-style. Grill quickly, close to coals, basting with marinade.

Serves 4.

Fish

Fish

Out of the water and into the frying pan is the byword of most real fisherman. A brief visit to your local fish market can remind you of lazy fishing days, too. Small whole fish and most fillets are best when grilled in special hinged wire baskets, which are relatively inexpensive and well worth owning if you like the wonderful flavor of fish cooked out-of-doors. Firm fish steaks can be cooked directly on oiled grills. Be sure to use lots of butter or sauce, since fish is delicate and low in natural oils.

Slow and easy baked trout

Put a fish in the campfire coals as you go to bed. You'll enjoy this simple way for baked trout.

Clean several large fish; remove the heads. Sprinkle inside and out generously with salt and pepper. Roll each in heavy foil, folding in the ends, then wrap each foil package in 8–10 pages of thoroughly wet newspaper. Dig a hole for each fish deep enough to permit covering with 1-in. of soil. Bury the bundles and build a campfire over them that is big enough to stay warm all night. The next morning, remove the fish. Serve for breakfast.

Smoked trout

Absolutely wonderful!

6 dressed rainbow trout (1 lb. each), or other dressed fish, fresh or frozen (thawed)
1 c. salt
1 gallon water
¼ c. salad oil

Remove the head just below the collarbone. Cut along the backbone almost to the tail. The fish should lie flat in 1 piece. Clean and wash. Add salt to water and stir until dissolved. Pour brine over fish and let stand for 1 hour. Remove fish from brine and rinse in cold water. To smoke the fish, use a charcoal fire in a barbecue grill with a cover or hood. Let charcoal fire burn down to a low, even heat. Cover with wet hickory, apple, or mesquite chips. Place fish on well-greased grill, skin-side down, 4 in. from the smoking coals. Cover and smoke for 1 hour. Add more wet chips as needed to keep the fire smoking. Increase the temperature by adding more charcoal and opening the draft. Brush fish with oil. Cover and cook for 15 min. longer. Brush fish again with oil. Cover and cook for 10 min. longer or until fish is lightly browned.

Serves 6.

Open fire pan-fried fish

The traditional fisherman's method.

4 small trout, catfish, or
   perch, pan-dressed
salt and pepper to taste
¾ c. all-purpose flour
½ c. cornmeal
½ c. milk
2 T. butter or oil

Season fish generously with salt and pepper. Combine flour and cornmeal in a pan. Dip fish in milk, then in flour mixture to coat. Fry fish in hot butter in a large skillet over a medium heat for 4 min. on each side, until fish flakes when tested with a fork.

Serves 6.

Grilled sesame perch

Any small whole fish is good this way.

6 serving-size perch or
   other locally available
   fish, pan-dressed
½ c. lemon juice
4 t. salt
¼ t. pepper
¼ c. sesame seeds,
   toasted
¾ c. butter or
   margarine

Make 3 shallow slashes on each side of fish. Mix lemon juice, salt, and pepper. Add fish and turn to coat. Refrigerate, covered, for at least 3 hours, turning occasionally. Mix sesame seeds and butter; heat until melted. Pour marinade into sesame mixture. Put fish directly on grill or in large folding wire grill. Cook over medium coals, basting often with sesame sauce, for about 5 min. on each side, until fish flakes when tested with a fork.

Serves 6.

Barbecued catfish with bacon

2 lb. catfish, or other small fish, fresh or frozen (thawed), pan-dressed
2 T. lemon juice
2 t. salt
¼ t. pepper
1 lb. bacon, sliced

Clean, wash, and dry fish. Brush inside with lemon juice and sprinkle with salt and pepper. Wrap each fish with a slice of bacon. Place fish in greased, hinged wire grills. Cook about 5-in. from moderately hot coals for 10 min. Turn and cook for 10–15 min. longer, until bacon is crisp and fish flakes easily when tested with a fork.

Serves 6.

Simple salmon steaks

2 lb. salmon steaks, or other fish steaks, fresh or frozen (thawed)
2 c. Italian dressing
2 T. lemon juice
1 t. salt
pinch of cayenne pepper
parsley

Cut fish into serving-size portions. Place in a single layer in a shallow baking dish. Combine remaining ingredients except parsley; pour over fish and let stand for 30 min., turning once. Reserve sauce. Place fish on greased grill. Cook 4-in. from moderately hot coals for 8 min. Baste with sauce. Turn carefully and cook for 7–10 min. longer, until fish flakes when tested with a fork. Garnish with parsley.

Serves 6.

Barbecued sole fillets

1 lb. sole fillets, fresh or frozen (thawed)
2 T. soy sauce
1 t. lemon juice
salt and pepper to taste
½ c. sour cream
½ c. fine bread crumbs
2 T. sesame seeds, toasted

Brush fish with mixture of soy sauce and lemon juice. Sprinkle with salt and pepper. Coat both sides with sour cream. Mix bread crumbs and sesame seeds and roll fish in mixture. Broil fish in oiled wire basket over medium coals for 10 min., turning once.

Serves 2–4.

Oriental swordfish steaks

2 lb. swordfish steaks,
   or other fish steaks,
   fresh or frozen
   (thawed)
¼ c. orange juice
¼ c. soy sauce
2 T. chili sauce
2 T. melted butter or oil
2 T. parsley, chopped
1 T. lemon juice
1 clove garlic, finely
   chopped
½ t. oregano
½ t. pepper

Cut fish into serving-size portions. Place in a single layer in a shallow baking dish. Combine remaining ingredients, pour over fish, and let stand for 30 min., turning once. Reserve sauce. Place fish on greased grill. Cook about 4-in. from moderately hot coals for 8 min. Baste with sauce. turn carefully and cook for 7–10 min. longer, until fish flakes when tested with a fork.

Serves 6.

Halibut steaks aux herbes

2 lb. halibut steaks, or
   other fish steaks,
   fresh or frozen
   (thawed)
¼ c. white wine vinegar
¾ c. bottled clam juice
¾ c. melted butter or oil
⅓ c. lemon juice
2 T. chives, chopped
2 t. salt
1 clove garlic, finely
   chopped
¼ t. marjoram
¼ t. pepper
¼ t. thyme
⅛ t. sage
⅛ t. hot pepper sauce

Cut fish into serving-size portions. Place in a single layer in a shallow baking dish. Combine remaining ingredients, pour over fish, and let stand for 4 hours, turning occasionally. Reserve sauce. Place fish on greased grill. Cook about 4-in. from moderately hot coals for 8 min. Baste with sauce. Turn carefully and cook for 7–10 min. longer, until fish flakes when tested with a fork.

Serves 6.

Camptown fish fry

2 lb. red snapper fillets, or other fish fillets, fresh or frozen (thawed)
⅓ c. milk
1½ t. salt
dash of pepper
½ c. flour
¼ c. yellow cornmeal
1 t. paprika
pinch of cayenne pepper
4 T. butter or oil

Cut fish into serving-size portions. Combine milk, salt, and pepper. Combine flour, cornmeal, paprika, and cayenne. Dip fish in milk mixture, then roll in flour mixture. Fry in hot butter in a heavy frying pan about 4-in. from hot coals for 4 min. Turn carefully and fry for 4–6 min. longer, until fish is brown and flakes when tested with a fork. Drain on paper towels.

Serves 6.

Quick smoked fish bake

You can do this on a gas or electric grill and still get that smoky flavor.

2 lb. fish fillets
salt and pepper to taste
1 lemon, thinly sliced
¼ c. butter, melted
1 clove garlic, minced
1–2 t. liquid smoke

Season fish generously with salt and pepper. Arrange half the lemon in a shallow baking pan, add fish in single layer, then top with remaining lemon. Mix butter, garlic, and liquid smoke and pour over fish. Place pan on grill, close hood, and cook for 25–30 min. Baste frequently. Serve with the lemon slices and butter sauce.

Serves 6.

Barbecued cod fillets

2 T. onions, chopped
1 clove garlic, finely
   chopped
2 T. melted butter or oil
1 can (8 oz.) tomato
   sauce
2 t. lemon juice
½ t. salt
¼ t. oregano
3 drops hot pepper
   sauce
dash of pepper
2 lb. cod fillets, or other
   fish fillets, fresh or
   frozen (thawed)

Cook onions and garlic in butter until tender. Add remaining ingredients except fish, simmer for 5 min., stirring occasionally, and cool. Cut fillets into serving-size portions. Place fish in a single layer in a shallow baking dish, pour sauce over fish, and let stand for 30 min., turning once. Reserve sauce. Place fish in greased hinged wire grill. Cook about 4-in. from moderately hot coals for 8 min. Baste with sauce. Turn carefully and cook for 7−10 min. longer, until fish flakes when tested with a fork.

Serves 6.

Fish fillets in foil

Especially good if you don't own a fish grill basket.

2 lb. cod fillets, or other
   fish fillets, fresh or
   frozen (thawed)
2 green peppers, sliced
2 onions, sliced
¼ c. butter or
   margarine, melted
2 T. lemon juice
2 t. salt
1 t. paprika
dash of pepper

Cut fish into serving-size portions. Cut 6 pieces of heavy aluminum foil (12 x 12 in.) and grease lightly. Place 6 portions of fish, skin-side down, on foil. Top with green pepper and onions. Combine remaining ingredients and pour sauce over fish. Fold foil over and close all edges with tight double folds. Grill packages about 5-in. from moderately hot coals, for 45−60 min., or until fish flakes when tested with a fork.

Serves 6.

Catfish kebobs

2 lb. catfish fillets, or other fish fillets, fresh or frozen (thawed)
⅓ c. spicy lemon marinade (p. 19)
3 large, firm tomatoes, cut in sixths
1 can (1 lb.) whole potatoes, drained
1½ t. salt
dash of pepper
⅓ c. melted butter or oil

Skin fillets and cut into strips (1x4-in.). Place in a shallow baking dish, top with marinade, and let stand for 30 min. Reserve marinade. Roll fillets. Alternate fish, tomatoes, and potatoes on skewers. Place kebobs in greased hinged wire grills. Mix butter, salt, pepper, and remaining marinade and baste kebobs. Cook about 4-in. from moderately hot coals for 4–6 min. Baste with sauce. Turn and cook for 4–6 min. longer, until fish flakes when tested with a fork.

Serves 6.

Barbecued fish-stick sandwiches

Turns ordinary fare into a great meal.

¼ c. butter or margarine, melted
2 T. lemon juice
1 pkg. (8 oz.) frozen breaded fish sticks
5 frankfurter buns, split and toasted
⅓ c. blue cheese barbecue sauce (p. 17)

Dip frozen fish in mixture of butter and lemon juice, coating all sides. Grill in wire broiler basket over hot coals for 5–7 min., brushing with lemon butter and turning once. Spread sauce on hot buns and place 2 fish sticks in each.

Serves 5.

Salmon barbecue

Double or triple recipe for a big picnic.

1 can (14–16 oz.)
  salmon, drained,
  liquid reserved
½ c. onions, chopped
2 T. olive oil
½ c. celery, chopped
½ c. green pepper,
  chopped
1 c. ketchup
1 c. water
2 T. brown sugar
2 T. vinegar
2 T. Worcestershire
  sauce
1 t. prepared mustard
½ t. salt
dash of pepper
6 hamburger rolls, split
  and toasted

Break fish into large pieces. In a large kettle over hot coals, sauté onions in oil until tender. Add remaining ingredients except salmon and rolls. Simmer, uncovered, for 20 min., stirring frequently. Add salmon and simmer 10 min. longer, stirring frequently. Place ½ cup salmon mixture in each roll.

Serves 6.

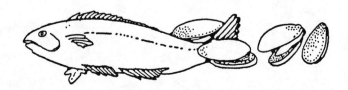

Shellfish

Shellfish

From simply grilled oysters to the major production of an authentic New England clambake (we also give you a simplified version), shellfish is the basis of some of the most elegant and most traditional cookout fare. Shrimp and scallops make particularly good kebobs, which are quick, easy, and festive.

Traditional New England clambake

A lot of work, but worth it for a party! Add some steamed lobster for a real treat.

4 broiler-fryer chickens
(2½ lb.), cut up
6 dozen steamer clams
12 medium sweet
potatoes
2 dozen ears of corn in
husks

At the beach, dig a pit (1 x 3½ feet) in the sand. Line it with dry flat rocks (about 6-in. wide). Using wood, build a fire on the rocks. Keep it burning for 1½–2½ hours. At the same time, wash 3 bushels of rock seaweed. Wrap individual servings of chicken in cheesecloth. Clean clams and sweet potatoes. Remove and save outer husks from corn. Pull back inner husks, remove silk, then re-cover with inner husks.

When stones are white hot, shovel embers from the pit and line with 6-in. seaweed. Cover seaweed with chickenwire (about 3⅓ feet square). Quickly layer chicken, potatoes, corn, and clams, separating them with seaweed. Top with corn husks and sprinkle with salt water. Immediately cover completely with a wet tarpaulin (5 x 5 feet or larger), anchoring it in place with large rocks. Steam food for 1 hour. If tarpaulin billows, unfasten a corner and allow steam to escape. Cook until chicken is tender and clams opened. Serve clams first. Follow with corn, potatoes, and chicken. Garnish generously with butter or margarine and salt and pepper. Have a large supply of napkins handy. Watermelon is a traditional dessert.

Serves 12.

Simplified New England clambake

6 dozen steamer clams,
cleaned
12 small onions, peeled
and parboiled
6 medium baking
potatoes, cleaned and
parboiled
6 ears of corn in the
husks, silk removed
6 live lobsters (1 lb.
each)
seaweed (optional)
lemon wedges
butter or margarine,
melted

Cut 12 pieces of cheesecloth and 12 pieces of heavy aluminum foil (18 x 36-in.). Place 2 pieces of cheesecloth on top of 2 pieces of foil. Place 2 onions, a potato, an ear of corn, a lobster, 1 dozen clams, and seaweed on cheesecloth. Tie opposite corners of cheesecloth together. Pour 1 cup water over the package. Make 6 packages by bringing foil up over the food and closing all edges with tight double folds. Place packages on a grill 4-in. from hot coals. Cover with hood or aluminum foil. Broil for 45–60 min. or until onions and potatoes are cooked. Open packages and crack lobster claws. Serve with lemon wedges and melted butter.

Serves 6.

Maryland clambake

The southern version of a Maine favorite.

6 dozen soft-shell clams,
cleaned
12 small onions, peeled
and parboiled
6 medium baking
potatoes, cleaned and
parboiled
6 ears of corn in the
husks, silk removed
12 live hard-shell blue
crabs
lemon wedges
butter or margarine,
melted

Cut 12 pieces of cheesecloth and 12 pieces of heavy aluminum foil (18 x 36-in.). Place 2 pieces of cheesecloth on top of 2 pieces of foil. Place 2 onions, a potato, an ear of corn, 1 dozen clams, and 2 crabs on cheesecloth. Tie opposite corners of cheesecloth together. Pour 1 cup water over the package. Make 6 packages by bringing foil up over the food and closing all edges with tight double folds. Place packages on a grill 4-in. from hot coals. Cover with hood or aluminum foil. Broil for 45–60 min. or until onions and potatoes are cooked. Serve with lemon wedges and melted butter.

Serves 6.

Grilled oysters

Messy and good.

36 oysters in the shell, cleaned
butter, melted

Place oysters on a grill about 4-in. from hot coals. Roast for 10—15 min. or until shells begin to open. Serve in shells with melted butter.

Serves 6.

Smoky oysters

A wonderful flavor!

Cook oysters in their own liquid until plump. Wrap in bacon, skewer and then grill until bacon is crisp.

Charcoaled scallops

2 lb. large scallops, fresh or frozen (thawed)
½ c. melted butter or oil
¼ c. lemon juice
2 t. salt
¼ t. white pepper
½ lb. bacon, sliced
green onions, minced

Rinse scallops with cold water to remove shell particles; place in a bowl. Mix butter, lemon juice, salt, and pepper. Pour sauce over scallops and let stand for 30 min., stirring occasionally. Reserve sauce. Cut each slice of bacon in half lengthwise and then crosswise. Wrap each scallop with a piece of bacon and fasten with a toothpick. Place in greased hinged wire grills. Cook about 4-in. from moderately hot coals for 5 min. Baste with sauce and sprinkle with onions. Turn and cook for 5—7 min. longer or until bacon is crisp. Garnish with onion.

Serves 6—8.

Scallop kebobs

Colorful and tasty.

1 lb. large scallops,
    fresh or frozen
    (thawed)
1 can (13½ oz.)
    pineapple chunks,
    drained
4 oz. mushrooms
1 small green pepper,
    cut into 1-in. strips
1 small red pepper, cut
    in 1-in. strips
¼ c. butter, melted
¼ c. lemon juice
¼ c. parsley, chopped
¼ c. soy sauce
½ t. salt
dash of pepper
12 slices Canadian
    bacon, cooked and
    halved

Rinse scallops with cold water to remove shell particles. Place pineapple, mushrooms, peppers, and scallops in a bowl. Combine butter, lemon juice, parsley, soy sauce, salt, and pepper and pour over scallop mixture; let stand for 30 min., stirring occasionally. Using long skewers, alternate scallops, pineapple, mushrooms, peppers, and bacon until skewers are filled. Cook 4-in. from moderately hot coals for 5 min. Baste with sauce. Turn and cook for 5–7 min. longer until bacon is crisp.

Serves 4–6.

Crab boil

Finger-lickin' good!

1½ gal. water
1 lemon, sliced
1 medium onion, sliced
½ c. seafood seasoning
    (Crab Boil)
⅓ c. salt
24 live, hard-shell blue
    crabs
butter, melted

Put water, lemon, onion, and seasonings into a large kettle. Cover and bring to the boiling point over hot coals. Plunge crabs into the boiling water. Simmer, covered, for 15 min. Drain. Serve with melted butter.

Serves 6.

Grilled blue crabs

Have the crabs cleaned at the fish store.

12 dressed blue crabs, fresh or frozen (thawed)
¾ c. parsley, chopped
½ c. melted butter or oil
1 t. lemon juice
½ t. soy sauce
dash of hot pepper sauce
lemon wedges

Clean, wash, and dry crabs. Place them in greased, hinged wire grills. Combine remaining ingredients, except lemon wedges, and heat. Baste crabs with sauce. Cook 4-in. over moderately hot coals for 8 min. Baste with sauce. Turn and cook 7–10 min. longer, until lightly browned.

Serves 6.

Lime grilled crab legs

Lemon juice is just as good.

½ c. butter or margarine, melted
3 T. lime juice
½ t. paprika
3 (12 oz.) pkg. precooked frozen king crab legs (thawed)
butter or margarine, melted
lime wedges

Combine butter, lemon juice, and paprika. Baste crab meat with sauce. Grill crab legs, flesh-side down, 4-in. over moderately hot coals for 5 min. Turn and baste with sauce. Heat for 5–7 min. longer. Serve with melted butter and lime wedges.

Serves 6.

Barbecued cheese-stuffed crab legs

3 (12 oz.) pkg.
   precooked frozen
   king crab legs
   (thawed)
4 oz. mushrooms, sliced
2 T. butter or oil
2 T. flour
½ t. salt
1 c. milk
½ c. Cheddar cheese,
   grated
paprika

Remove meat from shells, saving shells. Remove any cartilage and cut meat into ½-in. pieces. Cook mushrooms in butter for 5 min. Blend in flour and salt. Add milk gradually and cook until thick, stirring constantly. Add cheese and crab meat; heat. Fill shells with crab mixture. Sprinkle with paprika. Grill, shell-side down, 4-in. over moderately hot coals for 10–12 min.

Serves 6.

Cajun shrimp boil

1 gal. water
1 lemon, sliced
1 small onion, sliced
½ c. salt
½ c. seafood seasoning
   (Crab Boil)
1 clove garlic, sliced
5 lb. shrimp in the shell,
   fresh or frozen
   (thawed)
1 c. speedy barbecue
   sauce (p. 13)

Put water, lemon, onion, garlic, and seasonings into a large kettle. Cover and bring to a boil over hot coals. Add shrimp. Cover and simmer for 5 min. Drain. Serve with sauce.

Serves 6.

Shrimp kebobs

Also good with a scallop-and-shrimp combination.

2 lb. shrimp
1 c. soy sesame
   marinade (p. 19)
6 slices bacon

Marinate shrimp for 1 hour in sauce. Thread on skewer with 6 strips of bacon woven between. Broil until bacon is crisp and shrimp pink, about 5–10 min.

Serves 3–4.

Foil-barbecued shrimp

Easy and the sauce is in the bag!

⅓ c. butter or
   margarine
½ t. curry powder
1 clove garlic, minced
½ t. salt
pepper, freshly ground
½ c. parsley, snipped
2 lb. large shrimp,
   peeled and deveined

Blend all ingredients except shrimp. Divide shrimp onto 6 pieces of heavy aluminum foil. Top with butter mixture. Wrap foil around shrimp and seal well. Grill directly on hot coals for 5–7 min. Serve in foil.

Serves 6.

Fruit-glazed shrimp kebobs

2 lb. large shrimp
(14–15 per lb.),
fresh or frozen
(thawed)
18 wedges, lime or
lemon
½ c. apricot preserves
½ c. orange juice
½ c. lemon juice
¼ c. honey
1 T. cornstarch
3 drops hot pepper
sauce
1 t. chopped fresh or
dried mint, optional

Peel shrimp leaving tails on; remove veins and wash. Thread a lime or lemon wedge, 3 shrimp, a lime or lemon wedge, 3 more shrimp, and another citrus wedge on each skewer. Cover tails of shrimp with aluminum foil. Refrigerate, covered, until ready to cook. Combine preserves, orange and lemon juice, honey, cornstarch, and hot pepper sauce; stir until no cornstarch lumps remain. Cook until sauce thickens slightly, stirring constantly; simmer for 3–4 min. Broil kebobs on the grill for 5–10 min., until shrimp turns pink.

Serves 5–6.

Barbecued lobster

Kill the lobster by severing its spinal cord where the tail and main body shell meet (or have this done at the fish store). Slit the lobster along its bottom and remove the stomach, intestinal veins, liver, and coral. Place the lobster, slit-side up, on the grill and brush it with melted butter; sprinkle with salt and pepper. Grill slowly for 15–20 min., until slightly browned. Turn and cook for 10 min. more. Serve with melted butter.

Serve 1–1½ lb. per person.

Grilled lobster tails

Defrost 4 lobster tails. Remove the meat and cut into chunks. Marinate in ½ cup spicy lemon marinade (p. 19). Thread on skewer. Broil until pink.

Serves 4.

Vegetables and fruits

Vegetables and fruits

It is convenient that in the warm months, when most of us barbecue regularly, fresh, ripe, and delicious seasonal fruits and vegetables are at their peak. They take on new and exciting flavors when cooked over an open fire and complement beautifully grilled entrées of all types.

Foil-roasted corn

12 ears fresh corn
12 T. butter, softened
salt and pepper to taste

Remove husks and silk. Put each ear on a piece of heavy aluminum foil, spread with butter, and sprinkle with salt and pepper. Wrap foil, but don't seal seam. Grill over hot coals for 15–20 min., until corn is tender. Turn frequently. Serve with extra butter and salt.

Serves 8–12.

Barbecued corn-on-the-cob

12 ears fresh corn
⅔ c. classic uncooked
   barbecue sauce
   (p. 12)

Remove husks and silk. Put each ear on a piece of heavy aluminum foil, brush with sauce, and fold foil tightly over each ear. Grill corn over medium coals for 30 min., turning often.

Serves 8–12.

Indian roasted corn

4 ears fresh corn
salt
butter

Dampen husks with salted water. Grill ears over very low indirect coals for about 10 min. Turn to prevent burning. Remove husks carefully. Serve with butter and salt.

Serves 3–4.

Grilled potatoes in foil

baking potatoes
butter
chives, minced

Scrub and dry potatoes. Rub oil over surface. Wrap each loosely in aluminum foil, sealing ends with double fold. Grill for 1 hour, or until tender, turning several times. Cut an X in top of potatoes through foil and pinch open. Place butter in opening and sprinkle with chives.

Allow 1 per person.

Roasted spud slices

2–3 large potatoes, unpeeled, scrubbed, and sliced thickly
4–5 T. butter
chives, minced
parsley, minced

Overlap slices slightly on a sheet of heavy aluminum foil. Dot each with butter. Season with chives and parsley. Wrap foil tightly and place directly on coals for 1 hour or until tender, turning once.

Serves 2–4.

Seasoned potato grill

4 medium baking potatoes, scrubbed
onion salt
celery salt
pepper
4 T. Parmesan cheese, grated
4 T. butter

Cut potatoes lengthwise into ¼-in. slices. Divide into individual servings on pieces of heavy aluminum foil. Sprinkle each with onion salt, celery salt, pepper, and 1 tablespoon grated Parmesan cheese, covering all surfaces. Dot each with 1 tablespoon butter. Wrap foil and seal, leaving room for expansion of steam. Grill over coals for 30 min. or until tender, turning several times. Serve in foil.

Serves 4.

Herbed potatoes and onions

4 medium potatoes,
  thickly sliced
2 medium onions,
  thickly sliced
2 t. oregano
1½ t. salt
¼ c. butter or
  margarine

On a large sheet of heavy aluminum foil, mix first 4 ingredients and spread in a single layer. Dot with butter. Fold foil and seal ends. Put directly on top of medium coals and cook for 30–40 min., until potatoes and onions are tender, turning once.

Serves 4.

Grilled creamy potatoes

4 medium potatoes,
  peeled and thinly
  sliced
4 T. butter
4 T. Swiss cheese,
  shredded
salt and pepper to taste
8 T. milk

Lay slices in overlapping layers on a piece of heavy aluminum foil. Dot with butter and cheese; sprinkle with salt and pepper. Add milk. Fold foil and seal ends securely. Grill close to coals for 15 min. Open package to test for tenderness, reseal for longer cooking if needed.

Serves 4.

Barbecued eggplant

1 medium eggplant,
  sliced
¼ c. olive oil
salt and pepper to taste
1 clove garlic, minced

Soak eggplant in olive oil seasoned with salt, pepper, and garlic. Grill until brown on both sides.

Serves 4–6.

Picnic eggplant Parmesan

Great with barbecued veal chops.

1 small eggplant, cut
  into ½-in. slices
1 jar (15–16 oz.)
  meatless spaghetti
  sauce
½ t. salt
¼ t. pepper
½ pkg. (8 oz.)
  mozzarella cheese,
  thinly sliced
2 T. Parmesan cheese,
  grated

In metal-handled 10-inch skillet mix first 4 ingredients. Cook, covered, over medium coals for 20 min. or until eggplant is tender, stirring occasionally. Arrange mozzarella on top and sprinkle with Parmesan, then cover and cook until cheese is melted.

Serves 6.

Skewered zucchini

2 medium zucchini
¼ c. garlic marinade
  (p. 19)

Cut crisscross pattern over entire surface (⅛-in. deep). Cut in 2-in. chunks. Thread on skewers and grill for about 20 min., until tender yet crisp. Turn often and brush with garlic marinade.

Serves 4–6.

Barbecued bell pepper

1 green pepper,
  quartered
½ c. garlic marinade
  (p. 19)

Dip pepper strips in marinade. Place in hinged broiler and grill until edges are lightly browned.

Serves 2–4.

Vegetables and fruits

Grilled basil zucchini

Add some fresh tomato wedges if you wish.

6 medium zucchini, cut
   in ½-in. slices
½ c. onions, chopped
1 T. fresh basil, minced
1 t. salt
½ c. butter or
   margarine

On a large sheet of heavy aluminum foil or a
disposable aluminum cake pan, mix first 4 ingredients.
Dot with butter. Fold foil over and seal ends, or cover
pan with foil. Grill over medium coals for 25 min. or
until tender yet crisp.

Serves 8.

Potato-stuffed peppers

4 small sweet green or
   red peppers
¾ c. stiff mashed
   potatoes
½ c. Cheddar cheese,
   grated
2 slices crisp bacon,
   crumbled
salt and pepper to taste

Boil peppers for 2–3 min., cool, and remove stems
(reserve) and seeds. Mix potatoes, cheese, bacon, salt,
and pepper. Fill peppers with potato mixture and
replace tops securely. Wrap in foil and refrigerate. Grill
for 15–20 min. until heated through.

Serves 4.

Grilled onion slices

2 large mild onions,
   sliced thickly
butter, melted
salt and pepper to taste
parsley

Dip onions in butter. Broil on hinged grill until brown
on both sides. Season with salt, pepper, parsley.

Serves 4.

Foil-barbecued onions

4 small white onions,
   peeled
½ c. butter or
   margarine

Cut an X in end of each onion. Dot with butter, wrap tightly in heavy aluminum foil, and cook directly on coals for 30 min.

Serves 4.

Barbecued tomatoes

4 large tomatoes, halved
¼ c. spicy lemon
   marinade (p. 19)

Brush cut surface of tomatoes with marinade. Broil, cut-side up, on aluminum foil or greased grill over hot coals for 10 min. until heated through. Do not turn.

Serves 6–8.

Grilled stuffed tomatoes

4 medium tomatoes,
   halved crosswise
salt and pepper to taste
4 slices onion

Sprinkle salt and pepper on cut sides. Place halves together with onion between them; secure with toothpicks. Wrap in foil and grill for 20 min.

Serves 4.

Grilled mushrooms

12 large mushrooms
¼ c. butter, melted
salt and pepper to taste
paprika, minced

Dip mushrooms into butter. Grill until browned and heated through. Season with salt, pepper, and parsley.

Serves 3–4.

Quickie barbecued vegetables

Use any choice of vegetables you like.

1 pkg. (10 oz.) frozen
    vegetables
salt and pepper to taste
2 T. butter

Place frozen vegetables on a piece of heavy aluminum foil. Sprinkle with salt and pepper; place butter on top. Wrap foil and seal securely with a double fold; leave room for steam to expand. Place package on grill and cook for 10–15 min., turning occasionally.

Serves 3–4.

Summer vegetable grill

¼ lb. zucchini, cut into
    julienne strips
¼ lb. carrots (about 2),
    cut into julienne
    strips
½ lb. green beans, cut
    up
¼ lb. mushrooms, sliced
1 t. salt
½ t. oregano leaves
3 T. butter or margarine

Mix first 5 ingredients on a sheet of heavy aluminum foil. Spread in a single layer and dot with butter. Fold foil over vegetables and seal ends securely. Grill packet over medium coals for 1 hour or until vegetables are tender yet crisp.

Serves 4.

Vegetable kebobs

2 medium ears corn,
  husked and halved
12 cherry tomatoes
1 green pepper, cut into
  chunks
½ small eggplant, cut
  into chunks
1 c. garlic marinade
  (p. 19)

Place corn, tomatoes, pepper, and eggplant in a large bowl and top with marinade. Refrigerate, covered, for at least 1 hour, stirring occasionally. Drain vegetables, reserving marinade. Alternate vegetables on 4 skewers. Grill over medium coals for 20 min. or until tender. Turn occasionally and brush frequently with marinade.

Serves 4.

Vegetable kebobs

1 medium eggplant
  (about 1 lb.), cut into
  18–20 chunks (about
  1 x 1½-in.)
1 large cucumber, cut
  into 8–10 slices, ½-
  in. each
2 large green peppers,
  each cut into 8 pieces
3 zucchini, cut into 10–
  12 chunks, 1½-in.
  each
1½ c. spicy lemon
  marinade (p. 19)
¾ c. fresh herbed
  barbecue sauce
  (p. 13)

Toss vegetables with marinade in a bowl. Turn occasionally. Thread on skewers and grill over low coals until cooked through, about 10 min. Serve with sauce for dipping.

Serves 10–12.

Grilled peaches

Great with barbecued ham.

1 can (29 oz.) cling
   peach halves, drained
2 T. butter or margarine
3 T. brown sugar

In a skillet, melt butter and add brown sugar. Add peaches. Heat on grill, spooning mixture over peaches.

Serves 4–6.

Rotisserie whole pineapple

Great with pork chops.

1 medium pineapple
15–20 whole cloves
½ c. maple syrup
¼ t. nutmeg
¼ t. cinnamon

Pare pineapple but leave crown attached. Remove eyes and replace with cloves. Place pineapple on spit and secure with holding forks. Wrap crown in heavy foil. Rotate over hot coals for 45–60 min., basting often with mixture of remaining ingredients. Slice and serve hot.

Serves 4–6.

Accompaniments, snacks, and desserts

Accompaniments, snacks, and desserts

Round out your cookout meal without ever going into the kitchen. Here are some super ideas for breads, snacks, and even simple desserts to be cooked over your barbecue. Included are a sampling of the classic salads, most of which can be prepared well in advance. Use these in your meal planning for a total barbecue feast anytime.

Calico picnic slaw

½ c. sour cream
½ c. mayonnaise
1 T. sugar
1 t. salt
½ t. pepper
1 T. cider vinegar
½ t. dry mustard
1 T. salad oil
2 T. cream
2 hard-boiled eggs,
  chopped
3 c. red cabbage,
  shredded
3 c. green cabbage,
  shredded
1 c. carrot, shredded

Combine first 10 ingredients. Pour over cabbage and carrot. Mix thoroughly.

Serves 10–12.

Apple slaw

small head green
  cabbage (about 1½
  lb.), shredded finely
3 T. oil
salt to taste
pepper, freshly ground,
  to taste
2 medium carrots,
  peeled and grated
4 stalks celery, trimmed
  and cut in julienne
  strips
2 crisp red apples,
  peeled and sliced
2 T. white wine vinegar
½ c. sour cream or
  mayonnaise

Combine cabbage and oil and toss well until coated. Add seasoning and then remaining ingredients. Mix until well blended. Adjust seasoning.

Serves 6–8.

Hot German slaw

½ c. cider vinegar
⅓ c. water
⅓ c. sugar
½ t. salt
¼ t. black pepper
4 T. bacon drippings
1 egg
6 slices bacon, crisply
   cooked and crumbled
1 medium head green
   cabbage, shredded
   finely
1 medium onion,
   chopped

In a saucepan, mix first 7 ingredients and heat slowly. Stir until mixture comes to a boil. Immediately pour over cabbage and onion. Serve warm, topped with bacon.

Serves 6–8.

Layered potato salad

3 lb. potatoes, boiled,
   peeled while hot, and
   sliced thinly
¼ t. dry mustard
⅓ c. green pepper
   relish
4–5 slices bacon,
   crisply cooked and
   crumbled (drippings
   reserved)
1 T. vinegar
1 c. mayonnaise
1½ t. celery seeds

Layer potatoes in a serving dish, then sprinkle with dry mustard and 1 tablespoon relish. Top with a layer of bacon; moisten with mixture of vinegar and bacon drippings. Cover with a layer of mayonnaise and a sprinkling of celery seeds. Repeat layers until ingredients are used up, finishing with mayonnaise. Serve warm.

Serves 8–10.

Accompaniments, snacks, and desserts

Three bean salad

1 lb. can wax beans
1 lb. can green beans
1 lb. can red kidney
   beans, rinsed until
   clear
1 sweet pepper, chopped
1 sweet onion, thinly
   sliced
1 c. sugar
1 c. vinegar
½ c. salad oil
salt and pepper to taste
diced celery and
   pimento, if desired

Mix all ingredients. Let stand overnight.

Serves 8–10.

Garden salad

Great at most outdoor parties, particularly good with beef steak or hamburgers.

Break greens into bite-size pieces in a large bowl. Prepare a dressing of 4 parts oil to 1 part wine vinegar or lemon juice. Add salt and freshly ground black pepper to taste; also mustard, garlic, Worcestershire sauce, or herbs, if you wish. Pour over greens and toss at the last minute.

Variations. For a Caesar salad, add grated Italian cheese, bread cubes cooked in oil, and a raw egg to the dressing. Other possible additions include quartered tomatoes, sliced cucumbers, and sliced radishes; chilled shrimp and hard-boiled eggs; crisp bacon bits.

Allow about 1 cup per person.

Molded citrus salad

3 T. plain gelatin
½ c. cold water
1 c. boiling water
1 c. sugar
3 c. grapefruit pulp and orange juice (canned or fresh)
8 oz. whipped cream cheese
1 c. walnuts, chopped

Dissolve gelatin in cold water and dissolve sugar in boiling water, cool, and combine. Add grapefruit pulp and orange juice. Place half of mixture in a rectangular mold and refrigerate. When solidified, top with a mixture of cream cheese and nuts. Then, top with remaining half of grapefruit-and-gelatin mixture. Refrigerate until set.

Serves 8–12.

Barbecued bread sticks

½ t. hot pepper sauce
½ c. butter or margarine, melted
12 Italian bread sticks

Mix pepper sauce with butter. Roll bread sticks in mixture. Wrap in foil and heat on grill for 10 min.

Serves 6–10.

Garlic bread

½ c. butter or margarine, softened
2 cloves garlic, minced
1 long loaf Italian bread, cut in 1-in. slices with bottom crust uncut

With fork, mix butter and garlic in a small bowl. Spread garlic butter between bread slices. Wrap in foil. Grill over hot coals for 20 min.

Serves 6.

Herbed bread

6 T. butter or
margarine, softened
2 T. Parmesan cheese,
grated
2 t. Italian herb
seasoning
2 round loaf Italian
bread, halved
horizontally

Mix butter, cheese, and seasoning in a small bowl.
Spread cut sides of bread with mixture. Press halves
together and wrap in foil. Grill as above over hot coals
for 20 min. Slice into wedges to serve.

Serves 6.

Cheese-chive bread

½ c. butter or
margarine, softened
½ c. Cheddar cheese,
shredded
¼ c. chives, chopped
2 T. coarse-grained
mustard
1 round loaf (1 lb.) dark
rye bread

With fork, mix butter, cheese, chives, and mustard in a
small bowl. Cut bread into 12 vertical slices (¾-in.
thick), not quite through bottom crust. Spread mixture
into every other slice. Wrap in foil. Grill over hot coals
for 25 min. or until well heated.

Serves 6–8.

Rolls on a spit

12 brown-and-serve rolls
½ c. butter, melted

Thread rolls on a spit and brush with butter. Rotate
over coals for 10–15 min.

Serves 8–12.

Riviera bread

½ c. butter or
   margarine, softened
2 T. anchovies, minced
2 t. parsley, minced
1 t. lemon juice
1 long loaf French bread

In a small bowl, with spoon, mix butter, anchovies, parsley, and lemon juice. Halve bread lengthwise and spread cut sides with butter mixture. Reassemble and wrap in foil. Grill over medium coals for 15 min. until hot.

Serves 8–10.

Barbecued tidbits

12 cooked prunes
12 canned water
   chestnuts
12 slices bacon, halved

Wrap prunes and water chestnuts in bacon. Skewer and grill until bacon is crisp.

Serves 6–8.

Campfire popcorn

Heat ready-to-cook popcorn in its disposable container right on the grill. Add grated Parmesan cheese and melted butter.

Serves 2–4.

Barbecued peanut butter sandwiches

Make sandwiches with good white bread, peanut butter, and any jelly. Spread outsides lightly with soft butter. Grill, turning once, until hot. Cut each into 4 strips.

Allow one sandwich per person for a meal, 1–2 strips as a snack.

S'mores

The classic cookout dessert.

Toast 12 marshmallows. Sandwich 2 hot marshmallows and a piece of a milk chocolate bar between 12 graham crackers.

Serves 6.

Coated marshmallows

Skewer 12 marshmallows. Toast until golden. Dip in chopped nuts, shredded coconut, or chocolate sprinkles.

Serves 4.

Sweet and spicy popcorn

Heat corn in a covered skillet or wire corn popper. Sprinkle with sugar and cinnamon, using ½ teaspoon cinnamon and ¼ cup sugar for every 3 quarts popcorn.

Cookout apple pie

Use any other fruit pie of choice, but omit the cheese.

Place Cheddar cheese slices on top of a commercially baked apple pie. Cover loosely with foil. Grill until cheese melts.

Dessert kebobs

Alternate cubes of pound cake, marshmallows, and canned pineapple chunks on skewers. Grill until marshmallows begin to melt. Dip in hot fudge sauce.

Allow 2 pieces of cake, marshmallow, and pineapple per person.

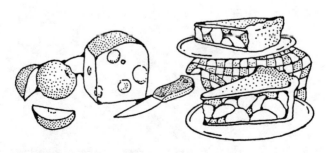

Nutty cake kebobs

Cut angel food cake into cubes (1½-in.). Using a fork, dip in melted currant jelly or sweetened condensed milk, then roll in chopped peanuts to cover. Skewer and toast over hot coals. Turn often until golden. Dip in chocolate sauce.

Allow 3 cake cubes per person.

Donut holes

2 pkg. biscuits,
   refrigerated
butter, melted
cinnamon
sugar

Cut biscuits in thirds and roll each piece into a ball. Place on skewers, leaving ½-in. between them. Brown over hot coals, turning constantly, for 7 min. Remove from skewers and dip in melted butter. Then roll in mixture of cinnamon and sugar.

Serves 6.

Waffles à la mode

Toast 6 frozen waffles on the grill. Top with vanilla ice cream. Drizzle with maple syrup or chocolate sauce. Top with chopped pecans.

Serves 6.

Hot fruit sundae

3 large peaches, cut in
  wedges
3 large bananas, cut in
  wedges
½ c. orange juice
½ c. sugar
2 T. brandy (optional)
3 pt. vanilla ice cream

Place fruit wedges and orange juice in a large saucepan
(preferably with a metal handle). Grill over low coals
for 10–15 min., until fruits are tender. Stir
occasionally. Remove from grill. Mix in sugar and
brandy. Serve over ice cream.

Serves 8.

Cookout cake

1½ c. packaged
  buttermilk baking
  mix
⅓ c. sugar
1 egg, well beaten
¼ c. milk
½ c. almonds, chopped
  and toasted

Line the bottom of a greased heavy skillet with 2
pieces of heavy foil; grease again. Blend baking mix
and sugar with a spoon in a medium bowl. Add egg
and milk and stir thoroughly. Pour into skillet and
sprinkle with almonds. Cover tightly and grill over low
coals for 20–25 min. (do not lift cover), until cake
springs back when pressed lightly.

Serves 6.

Accompaniments, snacks, and desserts

FREDERICK E. KAHN, M.D. is the general editor for the series of cookbooks to appear under the general title of "Preparing Food the Healthy Way."

Dr. Kahn, a practicing psychiatrist, brings to this series his interest and expertise in the essential nutritional and psychological aspects of personal health. In that vein, he is presently involved in a study of individuals who have suffered from Myocardial Infarction.

He is currently serving as an Assistant Attending Physician at both Columbia College of Physicians and Surgeons, and St. Luke's-Roosevelt Hospital in New York City, and is a member of the Harry Stack Sullivan Society of the William Alanson White Institute for Psychoanalysis.

He is a graduate of the University of Michigan and Wayne State University Medical School.

Index

OUTDOOR COOKING

PREPARING FOOD THE HEALTHY WAY SERIES
ORDER FORM

If you've enjoyed using this book, and would like copies of any other books in this series, indicate the *number of copies of each title* you wish to order, enclose a check or money order for the appropriate amount, and send in the entire page. Allow 6 weeks for delivery.

NUMBER
OF COPIES

____ Appetizers	____ Ground Meat
____ Beverages	____ International Meals
____ Breads & Cakes	____ One-Dish Meals
____ Breakfast & Brunch	____ Outdoor Cooking
____ Canning and Preserving	____ Party Cooking
____ Chinese Food	____ Poultry
____ Cooking With Kids	____ Sandwiches
____ Dessert	____ Sauces
____ Fish	____ Seafood
____ Fruit	

Please send me the books checked above. I have ordered ____ books at $4.95 each.

	NUMBER OF COPIES	PER COPY		
	X	$4.95	=	$
Plus postage and handling	X	.50	=	$
Total enclosed				$

Mail this form and your check to: Nautilus Communications, Inc., 460 East 79th Street, New York, NY 10021. No COD's, please!

Name _____

Address _____

City _____ State _____ Zip _____

Dear Reader:

We hope that you are enjoying this book, and that you have seen some of the other books in this series. If you would like to order additional titles, an order form is enclosed for your convenience.

Many of the recipes in this book have been provided by outside contributors. We are always looking for additional recipes and would welcome receiving your favorites for inclusion in future cookbooks.

If you would like to send us recipes, please use the form below. **Recipes must be typed.** *If your recipe is used, you will receive a free copy of the book in which it appears. If you need more forms, you may make photocopies of this one.*

Recipe name _____

Ingredients

_____ _____

_____ _____

_____ _____

_____ _____

_____ _____

_____ _____

_____ _____

Baking temperature _____

Directions _____

_____

_____

_____

Serving size _____ *List variations on back.*

Name _____

Address _____

City _____ *State* _____ *Zip* _____

Send your recipes to:
Nautilus Communications, Inc.
460 East 79th Street
New York, NY 10021